CHRIST-CENTERED
LEADERSHIP
AT WORK

CHRIST-CENTERED
LEADERSHIP
AT WORK

CALLED TO SERVE
ON MONDAYS

JIM DEVRIES & RICK SESSOMS

Published in the United States of America by Credo House Publishers, a
division of Credo Communications LLC, Grand Rapids, Michigan
credohousepublishers.com

ISBN: 978-1-62586-198-6

Cover design by Rob Monacelli
Interior design and layout by Frank Gutbrod
Editing by Jean Kavich Bloom and Vanessa Carroll

Printed in the United States of America

First edition

*To the gifted, Christ-centered leaders in Africa
and South Asia who, as this book is written,
labor to train succeeding generations of leaders
while facing the many new obstacles created
by the disruption of their world due to COVID-19.
The commitment and innovation they
demonstrate is inspiring.*

CONTENTS

PREFACE

JIM DEVRIES

Christ-Centered Leadership at Work is largely written in my voice, but Rick is indeed its coauthor as our combined leadership experiences, stories, and insights infuse these pages. God has allowed us both to serve Him in many organizations and levels of leadership responsibility, and in doing so, He's given us opportunities to reflect Him to others—the central focus of Christ-centered leadership.

Yet as fallible human beings, we've often failed. Reflecting Christ in the workplace, for leaders and followers alike, is an impossible task without continuously asking for the Holy Spirit's help every moment of every day. We've had that and much more to learn. Even as Christ-centered leaders, we've had to grow.

All that brings me to why we've written this book. Rick and I talked about how most studies attempting to determine the leadership style, characteristics, and personality traits of great leaders never seem to produce a clear profile. But perhaps, we thought, that's because they're looking at the wrong example. Then we wondered if God could use our stories and the lessons we've learned to not only show Christ is the ideal leader but what being a Christ-*centered* leader looks like and how to become one.

We came to the conclusion that He could. So we're sharing those stories and lessons for those of you who want to lead with Christ as your example. We don't claim to be perfect models, but you'll not only see that we've grappled with the same issues challenging you but how God helped us find our way when we focused on His ways.

What is our hope for this book? That it will help you become a more effective leader, reflecting Christ all along the way; understand that the focus of your leadership must be upward toward God and outward toward others; and make a significant, positive impact on those God gives you to lead.

INTRODUCTION: BEFORE WE BEGIN

The four parts of this book cover areas we believe will be helpful for you, whether you're determining if God is calling you to leadership, you're just starting out, or you're faithfully striving to be a Christ-centered leader in an ongoing quest.

Part I explores paths on a journey common to many leaders. Part II reveals how God has worked throughout my own life and leadership roles as an example of what He offers those of us who follow Him. Part III outlines the components Rick and I believe Christ-centered leaders can employ to best foster healthy cultures. And Part IV serves as both warning and encouragement.

Three additional pieces follow with the topics of responsible communication; learning from Jesus, the master communicator; and leadership as a layperson in the church.

But before we begin, I'll introduce you to three concepts foundational to everything in this book: (1) the significance of leaders as followers, (2) why who we are matters more than what we do, and (3) why reflecting Christ to those we lead is so significant.

FIRST FOLLOW, THEN LEAD

Jesus clearly stated that His first responsibility was to follow the will of His Father— "I have come down from heaven, not to do my own will but the will of him who sent me."

Think about this. Jesus followed His Father's will and became an exact representation of Him. And when His disciples asked Him to show them God, He answered, "Whoever has seen me has seen the Father." After more than four hundred years of silence, God had sent His Son to earth so the world could have a glimpse of the Father.

But then Jesus called His disciples to follow Him so they could become a picture of *Him*. If we are to be Christ-centered leaders, we must first be zealous followers of Jesus—not to be successful leaders in the world's eyes but to be reflections of Him.

The other day I went out with a group of friends for a Chinese meal. You know, egg drop soup, egg rolls, and crab puffs. I always look for the goodie they bring with the bill, and if it's a classy place, they often offer a fortune cookie *and* an almond cookie.

This time I got only a fortune cookie, which tells you something about my taste in restaurants. But the fortune in my cookie said, *A leader is a person you will follow to a place you wouldn't go by yourself.* In one aspect, the fortune cookie had it right—a leader must have followers. Having followers makes you a leader. But to be a Christ-centered leader, start by following Jesus.

You may wonder if Christ-centered leadership is the same as servant leadership since that term is often used to describe the way Jesus led—as a servant to His followers. Some observers do equate that style of leadership with Christ-centered leadership. But Christ-centered leadership differs. It's not about how a leader leads; it's about who the leader is. It's about following Jesus.

Christ-centered leadership, therefore, is not about self; it's about focusing on others. It's not about personal gain; it's about sacrifice. It requires us to focus on reflecting Jesus to others, cultivate character in both ourselves and our followers, value every individual as unique and special, and demonstrate a leadership style based on trust. In other words, Christ-centered leadership requires an absolute commitment to following Christ and His standards.

But here's the most significant difference: one can be a servant leader without a complete and vibrant commitment to Jesus. For example, God called King Nebuchadnezzar His servant even though the man was an agnostic.

Jesus did model servant leadership, and some Christ-centered leaders use servant leadership vocabulary to convey how they lead. Jesus and servant leadership are the subject of numerous books, articles, and sermons, morphing the concept into many different varieties. But most of them fall short in what we believe to be a critical component of Christ-centered leadership—being a follower, following Jesus.

WHO YOU ARE MATTERS THE MOST

The majority of books on leadership emphasize what leaders do and minimize who they are. And if you're a doer, like I tend to be, you probably believe you need to act in every situation you encounter. But God doesn't always call us to action as leaders; sometimes He calls us to watch Him perform.

In his book *The Path of Waiting*, Henri Nouwen explains that Jesus's ministry had two parts. For three years, He was active—healing the sick, casting out demons, and teaching His disciples, to give just a few examples. Then while in the garden of Gethsemane the night before His crucifixion, He prayed, "My Father, if this cannot pass unless I drink it, your will be done." Jesus allowed God to give Him up to those who intended to harm Him. Instead of being the one acting, He became a recipient of their actions.

The rest of His earthly ministry consisted of only a day, when He allowed others to revile and crucify Him. He was who He was, the Son of God. Christians today are virtually unaffected by Christ's active ministry, but His willingness to accept the abuse of a few, being who His Father made Him to be, makes eternal life possible for them.

Believe it or not, who we are really has more influence on our followers than what we may or may not do. That's why Rick and I want to convince you that you can best reflect Christ by who you are. God led me when I didn't understand His leadership and, sometimes, even when I was in desperate opposition to it.

I needed to learn that God's plan is for my followers to see Christ by who I am, not by what I accomplish.

WHY REFLECTING CHRIST IS SO SIGNIFICANT FOR WORKPLACE LEADERS

Here's why reflecting Christ is so significant for workplace leaders: God often allows them access to a wider cross section of people, giving them even more opportunity to touch lives that may never catch a glimpse of Christ otherwise.

For instance, many pastors have only Sundays to influence most of their parishioners, but your associates see you throughout the week. That means they observe not just what you accomplish but the authentic you. And that means they see all your struggles, bumps, bruises, and shortcomings as you steadfastly seek to serve your Lord each day.

Others aren't drawn to you because they think you're perfect, you know. Your faith despite your imperfections and your willingness to continue serving despite the obstacles you encounter draws them, giving you the opportunity to reflect Jesus.

Now that we've covered these concepts, let's move on to Part I, "God's Call to Work and Leadership."

PART I
GOD'S CALL TO WORK AND LEADERSHIP

If you think God may be calling you to lead, you probably have questions. And if you're already in a leadership position, we're sure you have questions—unless, that is, you're under the impression that you already know it all. But based on our own experiences, we have to ask—Do you?

You might also be dealing or have dealt with a couple of mistaken beliefs or experiencing a common fear, all of which can lead to decisions being questioned or regretted. Or maybe to decisions you're afraid to make.

Part I addresses all that as we explore God's call to leadership. Understanding the role and value of work itself, what God's call to work means and doesn't mean, and what a leader needs to be a leader are all part of becoming a Christ-centered leader.

FIRST, GOD'S CALL TO WORK

Before we can fully turn our attention to God's call to leadership and some of the barriers we might face in answering that call, we must first consider His call to work. Whether or not He calls us to be a leader, He calls us to make a difference in our world through our work.

As you'll see in Part II, God actively called me to different occupations for which He had previously trained me. Only recently did I begin to understand the theology of the doctrine of work, and now, looking back, God's purpose for my life is more apparent to me. I emphatically believe He called me to lead, but I also believe He first called me to work.

THE DOCTRINE OF WORK

The doctrine of work simply stated is *My faith and my work are inseparable*. We show faith through our actions in our workplaces, but to be faithful may require sacrifice. God may call us into an uncomfortable sphere of work that needs to be redeemed. There, we are to be salt and light—salt to preserve the good we find and light to expose the dark: "In the same way, let your light shine before others, so that they may see your good works and give glory to your Father who is in heaven."[1]

In chapter 4, we'll fully unpack the Bible's God-inspired, four-chapter gospel, which interacts with the doctrine of work. But for now know this: As a result of this interaction, God requires us to carry our light into all realms of our culture. The four chapters tell the story of how He will redeem all of His creation, and God fits our work into His story. Our vocation is not just about our happiness, fulfillment, or a plan. It's a beautiful and fantastic revelation of how God uses us to renew all things as part of His plan.

If we ignore any of these chapters, we minimize God. Each part is essential to His plan, and our work is essential because it reflects His glory.

Our work is also essential to God's plan to renew all things. We view the kingdom of God as existing in the future, but it's here now. The kingdom of God is the realm where Jesus rules here on earth and where we who trust in Him belong. The kingdom of God arrived when Jesus came to earth as a human, and after His second coming, it will appear in all its glory.

In 1 Corinthians, Scripture explains,

Each in his own order: Christ the first fruits, then at his coming those who belong to Christ. Then comes the end, when he delivers the kingdom to God to the Father after destroying every rule and every authority and power. For he must reign until he has put all his enemies under his feet.[2]

And in the book of Luke, we're told,

The Law and the Prophets were until John; since then the good news of the kingdom of God is preached, and everyone forces [is urged to find] his way into it.[3]

Author Paul Marshal reassures us that our work done for the kingdom of God will have enduring significance:

> Our works here and now are not all transitory. The good that we have done will not simply disappear and be forgotten. This world is not a futile passing phase; it will be taken up in God's new world. Our good buildings, our great inventions, our acts of healing, our best writings, our creative art, our finest clothes, our greatest treasures will not merely pass away. If they represent the finest works of God's image-bearers, they will adorn the world to come.[4]

And unlike man's evaluation, Jesus told us God values all work for eternity:

> "Do not lay up for yourselves treasures on earth, where moth and rust destroy and where thieves break in and steal, but lay up for yourselves treasures in heaven, where neither moth nor rust destroys and where thieves do not break in and steal. For where your treasure is, there your heart will be also."[5]

COMMON GRACE

Common grace is another gift of God that explains the ramifications of the doctrine of work. Common grace is God's grace by which He gives people, even His enemies, multiple blessings. Jesus said, "Love your enemies, and do good, and lend, expecting nothing in return, and your reward will be great, and you will be sons of the Most High, for he is kind to the ungrateful and the evil."[6]

He also said, "[My Father] makes his sun rise on the evil and on the good and sends rain on the just and on the unjust."[7]

God's common grace is apparent in the physical, intellectual, moral, and creative realms. As we work alongside our associates, God gives us unique opportunities to show Him through our actions. Common grace enriches the church through architects, musicians, builders, and artisans working together. God exercises common grace by postponing judgment until more people can enter into His kingdom. It is God using non-believers to protect His people.

Pharaoh's protection of Joseph in turn saved Egypt from starvation and provided shelter to the Israelites. God gives common grace to believers and unbelievers alike, and it is not a result of Christ's atoning work. Common grace gives a practical answer to why we can comfortably fulfill the cultural mandate by working alongside those who do not follow Christ.

Success is obeying God. Doing so pleases Him beyond all measure, outshining any earthly measure of success we may have achieved. Our obedience and not the "doing" is what's important. Our faithfulness in doing the work for God, not the nature of the work, is what brings Him and ourselves great joy.

PATHS TO LEADERSHIP

D o you wonder if you can really be a Christ-centered leader? Be encouraged! Your heavenly Father is fully aware of every obstacle you will face. He knows precisely the knowledge, abilities, and resources you need now and will need in the future. He will guide you, for "we know that for those who love God all things work together for good, for those who are called according to his purpose."[1]

That verse should give you confidence that God, through His Holy Spirit, is faithful to use your choices—good and bad—and the joys and frustrations you experience to make you more like Christ.

But what path to being a leader can you expect? We have news: it's different for everyone.

MY PATH

Dictators give commands and demand others carry them out, which leaves their followers no choice. Leading is demonstrating character and enabling your followers to do their tasks to the best of their ability. I believe God arranged a series of assignments to prepare me for the latter.

I started my first job when I was fourteen years old, working for Bernie in his corner grocery store. Bernie gave me directions and then left me alone to follow through. When I messed up, he showed me how to correct what I'd done the next time, all without a big fuss. As I learned, my responsibilities increased. For example, when I worked full-time during the summer, Bernie would transfer the responsibility for managing the produce department to me.

Bernie demonstrated how a true leader lead.

Later, I had other jobs with more responsibility. God enabled me to work for a wide range of talented and great leaders from Bernie to Art Collins, the COO of Medtronic Incorporated, a large multinational medical device company. I went from being responsible for two or three associates to being responsible for a large number of people and multi-million-dollar budgets.

I became a leader because God placed me where people offered me an opportunity to lead. My leaders consistently offered me more responsibility, and I responded to each new position.

RICK'S PATH

Rick's path to leadership is slightly different from mine. I never thought much about becoming a leader, but he began to form perceptions about leadership early in his life. And when Rick tells his story, he begins with a quote: "Children don't judge their own lives. Normal for them is what's laid before them day by day. Judgment comes later."[2]

Rick's father went to the University of North Carolina under the GI Bill to study accounting. Upon graduation, he became a Certified Public Accountant. As the years passed, he invested wisely in stocks and real estate. Both Rick's parents were successful and respected in the business community.

Rick's mother and father grew up in nominally religious homes, but then in their thirties they became more serious about their faith. Rick was eleven years old when the family set out in search of a Bible-believing church. Week after week they packed into a Rambler station wagon to visit yet another church, and this routine continued for months.

Then they were invited to a missionary convention across town. The first night the family showed up just as the proceedings started, and the only remaining seats were four pews from the front. Rick squeezed in between his father and the center aisle. The music was lively, and the missionaries, dressed in strange costumes, told exotic stories. Then the church's pastor stood to announce that an offering would be collected that night to buy a Jeep and a horse for the missionaries.

Rick says it was all a bit much for an eleven-year-old boy. On the drive home, he told his parents from the backseat, "I'm sure glad that's over." His father responded, "We're going back."

The next Sunday, he again sat next to his father as he made his first-ever missionary pledge, a faith promise to support the missionaries' work over the coming year. That church became their church, and what they learned there has impacted Rick's beliefs and choices over the past fifty years.

As a teenager in Sunday school, he learned that "only what's done for Jesus will last." Of course, the list of things that please Jesus the most, Rick was told, included praying, Bible reading, witnessing, and giving money. But the most significant of all was serving in full-time ministry.

And so Rick believed if he really wanted his life to count, he would have to surrender his life as a missionary to a foreign land. And if he couldn't make it to the mission field, the next best career option was to be a local church pastor. Otherwise, the teachers at the church told him, everything else he did in this life would end up in smoke and ashes when Jesus returned.

Rick says,

From the very first night I entered the doors of the church; it was crystal clear that missionaries were the heroes. The missionary convention was the most important week on the church's calendar. Each year missionaries would descend on the congregation with the latest news from Gog and Magog. They told stories of cannibal tribes who gave up their fetishes to follow Christ. They described traversing rickety bridges over rushing rivers in the jungles of Irian Jaya, evangelizing the "Orientals" in Hong Kong and preaching to thousands of Quechuas Indians high in the mountains of Ecuador.

These larger-than-life people ate around Rick's family's table. Rick slept on the couch while they borrowed his bedroom. When he was a teenager, they played basketball in the backyard with him. And when it came time for him to make a career choice, he decided to join their ranks.

Rick's parents were his greatest cheerleaders. They paid the bills while he went to Bible college, then to seminary. They waved a tearful good-bye when he and his wife, Tina, boarded the plane with their young children for a missionary assignment to Indonesia.

In Rick's home church he became one of those heroes. Whenever he and his family returned home on furlough, they were celebrities because Rick had pursued the "high calling." Rick and Tina were the ones doing "significant" work.

Meanwhile, the vast majority of those Rick knew as he grew up in the church had taken on roles as carpenters, auto technicians, computer analysts, homemakers, accountants, human resource managers, retail associates . . . They did not become celebrities. These peers became the supporting cast for the few who had chosen to pursue a high calling with their lives, like Rick.

Over the decades, Rick has been a missionary, local church pastor, and leader in various ministry organizations. A significant part of his work has been to motivate and mobilize the "laity" to fulfill the Great Commandment[3] and the Great Commission.[4] And through it all, just like He did with me, God was training Rick by giving him opportunities to lead.

OPERATING UNDER A MISTAKEN BELIEF

In the congregations he pastored, Rick emphasized the importance of being a good spouse and parent, how to evangelize and disciple neighbors, and how to be a good financial steward to support the ministry of others. But he was frustrated that men and women who spent so many hours at their mundane jobs didn't seem to make time for the vital work of ministry. In retrospect, that mind-set didn't reflect the New Testament emphasis on the "priesthood of all believers" (1 Peter 2:5–9).

How did the idea that missionaries and pastors have a higher calling than the vast remainder of Christ-followers come to dominate churches similar to the churches where Rick and I grew up?

We'll explore that in our next chapter.

CHAPTER THREE

MISTAKEN BELIEF #1

GOD VIEWS RELIGIOUS WORK AS HAVING THE MOST VALUE.

This first mistaken belief says work done in non-spiritual occupations is less meaningful than work done to serve God in a "religious" vocation such as pastor, missionary, or other professions the church has chosen to label "full-time Christian service."

Depending on your age and background, you may have heard the phrase *Only what's done for Jesus will last*. I heard it so often I believed it was a direct quote from the Bible. It's not! That phrase is a quotation from a hymn that began as a poem written by C. T. Studd— "Only One Life." This hymn reinforced this mistaken belief, and as a result, that belief has influenced succeeding generations as they searched for a vocation that pleased God. The first verse of the hymn is,

> Two little lines I heard one day,
> Traveling along life's busy way;
> Bringing conviction to my heart,
> And from my mind would not depart;

Only one life, 'twill soon be past,
Only what's done for Christ will last.

Singing this hymn regularly in church certainly encouraged this mind-set.

When was the last time you heard a sermon about the importance of any "non-spiritual" job to the building of God's kingdom? Have you ever heard a pastor or church leader say, "I think God wants you to serve Him in business?" Neither have I. But I'm convinced the Bible teaches that God values work in all shapes, kinds, and flavors equally with what some in the church have labeled full-time Christian service.

It took me years to understand this because it was counter to everything I'd learned. I went to a Christian school, and in junior high assemblies' week after week, we listened to a missionary tell a miraculous story about how God called him or her to the mission field. Wouldn't I like to do the same?

No, I wanted to be a farmer! But in church and Sunday school, I heard the message that full-time "religious" service was the only occupational choice God would bless. I heard it so often that I "tuned it out" and instead counted the number of ceiling tiles in the sanctuary.

When it was time for me to enter college, two of my brothers had decided to go into the ministry, and they were on their way to becoming heroes. My dad took me aside and said, "Jim, if you want to go into the ministry, I'll pay your tuition. Otherwise, you're on your own." God eventually led me to a vocation in biomedical engineering and blessed my work immensely. But I still struggled with occupational guilt as a result of my believing I should have answered to a higher calling—something "religious."

I wasn't alone with this feeling of guilt. Feeling as though you've missed God's call has burdened faithful followers of Jesus for years. Let me explain.

The origins of this faulty mind-set didn't start with a hymn written years ago; it started *thousands* of years ago. It took centuries for the church to develop it,[1] and it did so when it lost its theology of work.

Work was part of God's perfect creation before the fall: "The Lord God took the man and put him in the garden of Eden to work it and keep it."[2] The Lord also worked alongside the apostles as they spread the gospel: "They went out and preached everywhere, while the Lord worked with them and confirmed the message by accompanying signs."[3] Although we think of God ceasing His labors on the seventh day, Jesus said both He and the Father are still working.[4]

Recently, theologians have returned to writing about the theology of work. If you do an internet search on it or on the Reformation and work, you'll find many articles that give the history of the doctrine of work. I've found the work done by Hugh Whelchel to be some of the most thorough, and I've summarized the history he gives in his book *How Then Should We Work? Rediscovering the Biblical Doctrine of Work* in the following three paragraphs.

The early church's view of work gradually changed. During the first one hundred years, the church did not differentiate between the value of everyday work and work of a religious nature. Many of the church leaders were bi-vocational similar to Paul, who worked as a tentmaker.[5] Gradually, the emphasis on monasticism (monkhood) and the priesthood gave rise to the idea that sacred work was more significant to God's plan than secular work.

However, the Reformation placed a different emphasis on work. John Calvin, Martin Luther, and others helped Christians rediscover the biblical doctrine of work. Calvin taught that the individual believer has a vocation to serve God in the world and in every sphere of human existence, lending a new dignity and meaning to everyday work and opposing some of his contemporaries.

The church leaders, writers, and thought leaders in the Middle Ages despised work. They pointedly made the case that physical and other secular types of work were definitely of lower value. If you wanted to be truly spiritual, you shunned physical labor. The perfect Christian life was devoted to serving God, untainted by physical labor. Those who chose to work for a living were "second-class" Christians. Such attitudes reached their height at this time."[6]

For *First Things*, Alister McGrath wrote an article titled "Calvin and the Christian Calling."[7] He points out that underlying this new value of work proposed by Calvin is the notion of one's vocation or calling. Calvin believed that God calls His people not just to faith but also to express that faith in different areas of life. Whereas monastic spirituality regarded vocation as a calling out of the world into the desert or the monastery, Luther and Calvin regarded vocation as a calling into the everyday world. The idea of God's calling His people to a vocation by serving Him within His world was a radical departure from existing thought.

McGrath wrote,

> Jesus fulfilled His vocation by being called into this world. When we think about His saying "It is finished" on the cross, it's critical that we realize He did not merely mean He'd done all the things He wanted to do. He also meant He had allowed all the things done to Him to have fulfilled His vocation.[8] McGrath further explains that the Reformers saw work as a way Christians could deepen their faith.[9]

When Noah and his family came out of the ark, God told them He would never again curse the ground and that as long as the earth existed, there would be seedtime and harvest.[10] God values work in all spheres of human life.

He gave the plans to David for the temple,[11] assigned the work of building His temple to Solomon[12] and to Moses His tabernacle and its furnishings.[13] He gave the specifications for the priest's clothing and sent His spirit on Bezalel to provide him with skill, knowledge, craftsmanship, and the ability to do artistic designs.[14] And He called the musicians to celebrate with joyous noise and gave David the ability to write psalms of praise.[15]

As we reflect God to others around us, He wants us to glorify Him in every cultural and vocational sphere. We exalt Him through our work.

In his book *Business for the Glory of God*, Dr. Wayne Grudem says business is a neglected way to glorify God:

> When people ask how their lives can "glorify God," they aren't usually told, "Go into business." When students ask, "How can I serve God with my life?" they don't often hear the answer, "Go into business." When someone explains to a new acquaintance, "I work in such-and-such a business," he doesn't usually hear the response, "What a great way to glorify God!"[16]

Work in a non-spiritual occupation is not second-class. I believe that, for a true Christian, no occupation is non-spiritual. All legitimate work is a means for us to participate in the spread of God's common grace and to glorify our Father.

Go ahead. Discard the mistaken belief that says you must answer to a higher calling in your work. God gave all work to prepare us for ruling and reigning with Him for a thousand years.[17] Jesus said to His Father, "I glorified you on earth, having accomplished the work that you gave me to do. And now, Father, glorify me in your own presence with the glory that I had with you before the world existed."[18] And in the Old Testament, Daniel said,

"Go your way till the end. And you shall rest and shall stand in your allotted place at the end of the days."[19]

Next let's explore another mistaken belief that can be confusing—and wrong.

MISTAKEN BELIEF #2

IF I DON'T DO RELIGIOUS WORK, THE WORK I DO WILL BE SECOND-CLASS.

This mistaken belief says any vocation not directly related to spreading the gospel is second-class work. Where did that idea come from?

During the first half of the nineteenth century, the western world was experiencing the Second Great Awakening. (Led by several individual preachers, the best-known name at the start of the twenty-first century is probably American Charles Finney.) As a result of that awakening, the average evangelical Christian today focuses on a single issue that can be communicated in two "chapters."

As promised earlier in the book, we're going to unpack the four-chapter gospel—but after we explain the two-chapter gospel.

THE TWO-CHAPTER GOSPEL

The first chapter is "We have sinned." The second chapter is "We need to be saved from our sin." The second chapter contains God's solution to the problem presented in the first chapter. God sent Jesus into the world to reconcile us to Him through salvation made possible by Christ's life, death on a cross, and resurrection. We call this the two-chapter gospel.

The two-chapter gospel contains fantastic news, and every part of it is correct. But we've done a disservice to others by ignoring what the Bible teaches about creation and the end times. This results in the devaluation of work to a lower level than so-called full-time Christian vocations. As a result, we encourage potential leaders away from what many consider lower-level disciplines, which form the vast fabric of society. Think art, business, marketing, communications, and industry.

By having a myopic view of Scripture that focuses on a single issue in a complex world, we limit our ability to speak into other issues such as poverty, discrimination, and the disfranchised. We've ceded leadership in art, business, marketing, communications, and industry to others. In addition, we've almost ignored showing love to those whom God loves. Zechariah 7:9–10 says, "Thus says the LORD of hosts, Render true judgments, show kindness and mercy to one another, do not oppress the widow, the fatherless, the sojourner, or the poor, and let none of you devise evil against another in your heart."

The mistaken belief that says *If I don't do religious work, the work I do will be second-class,* which we've allowed to take root, needs to be corrected before we lose our ability to influence fields God states are important.

Moreover, the two-chapter gospel focuses on "self." It ignores other themes in the Bible—the creation of the heavens and the earth and the final restoration of God's creation. It leaves out God's reason for our creation and the Christian's final destination. Ultimately, salvation is not God's end purpose; His ultimate plan is to bring humankind and His renewed creation into a perfect relationship for eternity.

THE FOUR-CHAPTER GOSPEL

The complete story is called the four-chapter gospel, which consists of these four chapters: creation (how things should be); the fall (how things are), redemption (how things could be), and restoration or fulfillment (how things will be). In Genesis, God asks man, *Where are you?* And Revelation gives the answer to man's question, *Where is God?*

The four-chapter gospel emphasizes that God's work isn't complete until the restoration of His creation.[1]

Chapter 1: Creation—How Things Should Be
God created everything good (including work). In Genesis 1, the writer recounts the six days of creation. Here are some select verses:

> **On Day 1**, "God said, 'Let there be light. And there was light.' And God saw that the light was good" (verses 3–4).

> **On Day 2**, "God said, 'Let there be an expanse in the midst of the waters, and let it separate the waters from the waters.' And God made the expanse and separated the waters that were under the expanse from the waters that were above the expanse. And it was so. And God called the expanse Heaven. And there was evening and there was morning, the second day" (verses 6–8).

> **On Day 3**, "God said, 'Let the waters under the heavens be gathered together in one place, and let the dry land appear.' And it was so. God called the dry land Earth, and the waters that were gathered together he called Seas. And God saw that it was good. And God said, 'Let the earth sprout vegetation, plants yielding seed, and fruit trees bearing fruit in which is their seed, each according

to its kind, on the earth.' And God saw that it was good" (verses 9–12).

On Day 4, "God said, 'Let there be lights in the expanse of the heavens to separate the day from the night. And let them be for signs and for seasons, and for days and years, and let them be lights in the expanse of the heavens to give light upon the earth.' And it was so" (verses 14–15).

On Day 5, "God created the great sea creatures and every living creature that moves, with which the waters swarm, according to their kinds, and every winged bird according to its kind. And God saw that it was good" (verse 21).

On Day 6, "God created man in his own image, in the image of God he created him; male and female he created them . . . And God saw everything that he had made, and behold, it was very good" (verses 27–31).

According to Genesis, the "Book of Beginnings," God created all things very good. The first chapter of Genesis paints a beautiful picture of all creation, as it *should* be. When God originally placed Adam and Eve in the garden, He ordered them to "be fruitful and multiply and fill the earth and subdue it, and have dominion over the fish of the sea and over the birds of the heavens and over every living thing that moves on the earth."[2] He'd also delegated to Adam the task of naming the animals.[3]

With these tasks, God gave meaningful work to the first humans. Theirs was creative work because God, the ultimate creator, made them in His image. Therefore, meaningful work for Adam, Eve, and their descendants through the millennia has been an integral part of God's intention and design for the human race, flowing naturally out of His creative work. Jesus confirmed that "work" was necessary when He rebuked the Jews with these words: "My Father is working until now, and I am working."[4]

Chapter 2: The Fall—How Things Are

Sin entered the world when Adam and Eve partook the forbidden fruit. Sin impacted all things, including our work. Not only did their disobedience sever their fellowship with God and get them booted from the garden, but all aspects of God's created order suffered the fall's deadly effects:

- Fear and shame (Genesis 3:8–11)
- Strained relationships (Genesis 3:12)
- Serpents cursed (Genesis 3:14)
- Painful childbearing (Genesis 3:16)
- Enmity between men and women (Genesis 3:16–17)
- Increased difficulty of work (Genesis 3:17–19):

To Adam [God] said, "Because you have listened to the voice of your wife and have eaten of the tree of which I commanded you, 'You shall not eat of it,' cursed is the ground because of you; in pain you shall eat of it all the days of your life; thorns and thistles it shall bring forth for you; and you shall eat the plants of the field. By the sweat of your face you shall eat bread, till you return to the ground, for out of it you were taken; for you are dust, and to dust, you shall return."

Although our creator designed us for work, the fall profoundly impacted the difficulty by which we get our daily sustenance. Rather than having fruit for the taking, we battle thorns and thistles, and there's a lot of sweat in the daily grind. Our work was profoundly affected by the fall—a tragic picture of how things *are*.

Chapter 3: Redemption—How Things Can Be

Jesus lived, died, and rose again to set in motion the reconciliation of all things to the Father, including our work.

One day early in Jesus's earthly ministry, He unrolled the scroll of Isaiah and read the prophetic words that outlined His ministry of redemption. Jesus quoted from the Old Testament when He said this is why He came— "to proclaim liberty to the captives and recovering of sight to the blind, to set at liberty those who are oppressed, to proclaim the year of the Lord's favor."[5]

The apostle Paul's view of redemption, as he explained in Colossians,[6] led him back to Christ's lordship over all creation. Moreover, he said, someday "all things" will be reconciled to God through Christ the coming King. Jesus's sacrifice on Calvary made it possible for all things to be made new.

Indeed, Jesus came "to seek and to save the lost."[7] But He was about more than sin management. The gospel Christ proclaimed is cosmic in scope. A primary purpose of His work on the cross was the salvation of people, but He also came to resurrect thriving cities and neighborhoods.

This view of the gospel reframes our responsibilities. No longer do we narrowly define it as getting people into heaven, because redemption impacts our calling for the here and now. Not only are people to be redeemed, but all of creation is on God's heart. As a result, He calls us to play a role in the redemption of science, art, ethics, family and marriage, health, history, work, leisure, imagination, ecology, academics, worship, language, relationships, and more—for God created it all. He desires that all creation again more fully reflect who He is.

Romans 8:20–22 says,

> The Creation was subjected to futility, not willingly, but
> because of him who subjected it, in the hope that the

creation itself will be set free from its bondage to corruption and obtain the freedom of the glory of the children of God. For we know that the whole creation has been groaning together in the pains of childbirth until now.

The practical implications of this principle are legion. This view of the gospel implies that Christ's ambassadors of reconciliation should not avoid sexuality but sanctify it. Emotions should not be repressed but purified. The study of medicine must be transformed to become life-giving. Politics should not be declared off-limits but reformed. Art ought not to be pronounced worldly but claimed for Christ. Relational conflict should not be forfeited to those in power but redeemed by Jesus's reconciling agents. The workplace must not be despised as a necessary evil but engaged once again to conform to God-honoring excellence.

Jesus's work of redemption made it possible for all creation to be what it can be once again.

Chapter 4: *Fulfillment—How Things Will Be*

Finally, chapter four is a future vision of how all creation will someday be, "for in him all the fullness of God was pleased to dwell, and through him to reconcile to himself all things, whether on earth or in heaven, making peace by the blood of his cross."[8]

In the New Jerusalem, all things will be made new, including our work. In the book of Revelation, John describes it:

Then I saw a new heaven and a new earth, for the first heaven and the first earth had passed away, and the sea was no more. And I saw the holy city, new Jerusalem, coming down out of heaven from God, prepared as a bride adorned for her husband. And I heard a loud voice from the throne saying, "Behold, the dwelling place of God is with man. He will dwell with them, and they will be his people, and God himself will be with them as their God.[9]

God's unfolding drama, which began in a garden, will end in a city in a new garden. Death shall be no more. There will be no more mourning or crying or pain. God's plan to dwell with His people will again be a glorious reality. The final chapter is a picture of how all things *will be.*

The four-chapter gospel encourages Christ-followers to contribute powerfully to the purposes of God in their work. Armed with a perspective that God is reconciling all things to Himself, ambassadors of reconciliation spread throughout the workplace play a dramatic role in this unfolding drama.

WORKING WITH EXCELLENCE IN BABYLON

Rick first expressed these thoughts in an article titled "Leading with Excellence in Babylon," but they reflect truth for any who work, not only leaders.[10]

At times, the day-to-day grind of the workplace seems futile. The Old Testament prophet Daniel could have attested to that reality in spades. He had every right to wallow in self-pity, thinking his life was a waste.

Most of us have a faulty conception of Daniel's days, as though they're scenes from a prime-time flick with him hanging out in the lions' den, interpreting King Nebuchadnezzar's dreams, receiving historic prophetic visions, and seeing the handwriting on the wall. But all these experiences made up a tiny part of his work life. Most of his days, week after week, month after month, and year after year were spent much like ours—with daily routines. He also had a pretty awful job. After all, he was a slave, his owner the despicable king of Babylon.

So Daniel spent his workdays laboring in a monotonous government bureaucracy, with his coworkers a sorry lot—sorcerers surrounded him. For his entire adult life, he worked improving a nation that had devastated his hometown, Jerusalem. It would be hard to overstate the futility of Daniel's job. He spent his whole career building up an empire that God prophesied He would destroy. Daniel spent a lifetime on a project that would ultimately amount to nothing.

The mind-boggling part of Daniel's story is that God instructed Him and other exiles to work hard to build up Babylon and make it prosper:

> Thus, says the LORD of hosts, the God of Israel, to all the exiles whom I have sent into exile from Jerusalem to Babylon: Build houses and live in them; plant gardens and eat their produce. Take wives and have sons and daughters; take wives for your sons, and give your daughters in marriage, that they may bear sons and daughters; multiply there, and do not decrease. But seek the welfare of the city where I have sent you into exile, and pray to the LORD on its behalf, for in its welfare you will find your welfare.[11]

So Daniel obeyed, didn't complain, and pursued excellence with uncommon zeal. He was a man whose confidence was in God.

In his book *Significant Work*, Paul Rude wrote,

> The daily grind of our lives leaves far more than a tiny fingerprint on eternity. It strikes cosmic hammer-blows that forge the very shape of eternity. God pulls the white-hot ingot of eternity from the forging fire of His sovereignty. Then, like Master to apprentice, he entrusts

the hammer to our hands. He says, "Strike it. Strike it right here. This is your place. This is where I want you to shape eternity. Live the life I gave you to live." And so, in stammering awe, we take up the hammer. We live our lives, our regular everyday toilsome lives. The hammer falls. Sparks fly. Eternity bends, and the Master is delighted.[12]

Daniel saw sparks fly on the white-hot ingot of God's eternal masterpiece. Daniel invested himself fully into his work because he knew he was fulfilling the assignment God planned for him in the unfolding drama of eternity. God put him there, and God commissioned him to shape the future from this place, to play the hand God had dealt him in the reconciliation of all things to God through Christ.

Daniel's book concludes with God's ringing words, "Go your way till the end. And you shall rest and shall stand in your allotted place at the end of the days."[13] Thousands of years later, these words also ring true as we head to work on Monday morning. In them, we find the ultimate meaning of our daily work. The glory of God makes whatever we do significant as He assigns us our place in the four-part drama He's fulfilling. When we view and do our work from that perspective, no job is ever small or mundane or futile. Instead, we see all creation as it should be, reality as things are, redemption as all things can be, and the New Jerusalem once all things are made new. And so, every day in our work, we can see sparks fly.

But if you're also a potential leader, you'll want to know what pursuing that role will take. That leads us to our next chapter.

CHAPTER FIVE

WHAT A LEADER NEEDS TO BE A LEADER

A re you still wondering if you have what it takes to be a leader, either because you're having trouble seeing it or you feel like you've already failed at leadership?

We want to ask you two questions:

1. Do you have a Gideon Complex?
2. Do you have zeal?

THE GIDEON COMPLEX

Depending on a wide range of reasons, you might believe you don't have what it takes to be a leader. You might think no one will follow you. Worse, you might think you're not worthy of being a leader. This feeling can come from events during your childhood or previous failures made as a leader—sins you "know" God has not forgiven. Or your fear can come from cultural factors. You may have been raised "on the wrong side of the tracks" and think you're of the wrong social class.

I nicknamed this fear the Gideon Complex. When God called Gideon to free Israel from the power of the Midianites, Gideon replied, "Please, Lord, how can I save Israel? Behold, my clan is the weakest in Manasseh, and I am the least in my father's house."[1] If you're asking a similar question, you're not alone; even Moses argued with God's call at the burning bush: "Moses replied to God, 'Who am I that I should go to Pharaoh and bring the children of Israel out of Egypt?'"[2]

Everyone thinks they know what a leader should look like, but too often they make wrong assumptions. Assuming business headlines about the characteristics of a leader are correct is also a mistake. The leaders who get the most publicity are usually self-focused, arrogant, and seemingly successful. But it's easy to believe that if you don't have these same characteristics, you can't become an effective leader.

Leaders are human. No one can live up to all the qualifications they think they need to lead. Most leaders learn to be leaders by initially leading in a controlled environment. They make mistakes but have a continued desire to learn. No one starts at the top. Many who have the potential to be great leaders eliminate themselves from even trying because they mistakenly assume, they aren't qualified or don't have the "right" personality traits.

According to Jim Collins in his book *Good to Great*, the only two characteristics that make someone an outstanding leader are personal humility and the will to succeed.[3] But let me add to that:

You need to trust God. And you need zeal.

THE ROLE OF ZEAL

Ask yourself if God has given you a zeal for leading. The word *zeal* is not a common word, so let's take a moment to review its definition. Zeal means you have a great deal of energy or enthusiasm to pursue a cause or an objective. It's not transient, because it's an "in your bones" commitment that's part of you. It's a gift from God that verifies His desire for you to pursue an objective.

Zeal always trumps a grade point average. Once I was out of college, no employer ever asked me what my grade point average was. An employee who exhibits zeal for his work outperforms his contemporaries every time. The apostle Paul urged those who lead to do so with zeal.[4]

I owned two businesses. One dealt primarily with the design and development of devices for open-heart surgery and was extremely successful. I sold that business and purchased a furniture manufacturing company that, by comparison, was a disaster. Looking back, one of the reasons the medical device company was successful was that I had a zeal for that area of business. I did not have the same zeal for the furniture business. I had an interest in it, but it was never as compelling as my zeal for the medical industry.

Other factors were involved, of course, and I'll share more detail in Part II when I tell my story. But one difference was my lack of zeal for the second opportunity.

When I was beginning a search for the vocation God had in mind for me, I took a series of aptitude tests. Dead last was mechanical engineering. Yet God led me in such a way that I ended up graduating from college with a Bachelor of Science in that field.

God is writing the story of your life. Has He given you zeal for leading? Being a leader is not an easy road, and it requires a firm and steadfast commitment. Look at the "defining moments" God has given you. Can you see a pattern, indicating He's preparing you to lead? Moments that have given you the zeal you'll need.

If not (or you don't want to make a significant commitment for personal or family reasons), perhaps you shouldn't pursue a leadership position. Trust that God will instead lead you to the place or places He *has* prepared for you. If God intends you to be a leader, if you trust Him, if He's given you zeal—and especially if you're

willing to take developing as a Christ-centered leader seriously—
you're on your way.

Just don't believe you're not worthy or fear you will disappoint
God. As you read my story, you'll discover that at least at one point,
I felt I had failed God. Then through His abundant grace and
steadfast love, He showed me that was not the case.

The book of Isaiah, God's suffering servant, has much to say
about leadership as a servanthood—Christ-centered leadership as I
understand it. John N. Oswalt says this:

> [In Isaiah,] chapters 36–39 ask this question: What about
> my sinfulness and fallibility? Am I worth anything as a
> servant; would God even care to use me? Or am I, like
> Isaiah, simply undone by the uncrossable gap between
> the tinsel of human glory and the terrifying blaze of
> God's glory? Thus the chapters form a pivotal point
> between the revelation of God's glory and the revelation
> of his grace, both in its need and its availability.[5]

Oswalt goes on to say,

> Perhaps better than any single biblical book, [Isaiah]
> reveals the name and nature of the God who invites us to
> be his servants. He is holy, he is just, he is steadfast love.
> He is glorious, he is terrible, he dwells with the lonely
> and contrite. He is faithful, he is forgiving, he demands
> perfection. He is passionate, both loving right and hating
> evil. He calls us to lay aside our independence and trust
> in him, for he has chosen us and redeemed us in Christ
> and will *empower us* to be like himself."[6]

PART II
ONE LEADER'S JOURNEY

In this part of the book, I share my life story to illustrate the way God has faithfully woven my small decisions and my experiences together, then integrated my life with others' lives as a part of His grand plan. When I look back on all that's happened, my story encourages me, and I hope it will inspire you.

In the Bible, some journeys divide into three stages, commonly called orientation, disorientation, and reorientation. They are described by Walter Brueggemann in his book *The Message of the Psalms*,[1] and they are a way of explaining how God develops us spiritually. The journey begins with the orientation part of the cycle. This is a comfortable time, and we think we understand what is happening to us. Our faith is developing.

But then we bump into a time of disorientation. Everything in our lives is suddenly in a state of flux. We're stressed on many fronts, and our faith is challenged. We may struggle with doubt, fear, and searching for answers, or in my experience, sometimes unexpected blessings.

Then at the appropriate time, God brings us into a reorientation phase. Life and faith again begin to make sense. We typically emerge with a new and deeper perspective on our relationship with our Lord, our world, and ourselves! Each cycle can be days, weeks, or several years. There may be mini cycles within the longer cycles. Sound chaotic? It is, but God is stirring things up to guide us into a deeper relationship with Him.

The exodus journey, for the Israelites, started with an orientation period in Egypt, then leaving Egypt after four hundred years began a disorientation period. The reorientation period began when the Israelites entered the promised land.

Another example of this cycle is the pattern in the apostle Paul's life. It began as a time of orientation when, as Saul, he vigorously persecuted the new Christians. Disorientation occurred when Jesus confronted him on the way to Damascus. His time spent ministering to the Gentiles was a period of reorientation.

I see a similar pattern in my own life story, and that is how I structure it's telling in the following chapters. Perhaps your story has taken the same path—or will. But remember this: God is always there.

As you read my story, I want you to continue to come back to this verse: "We know that for those who love God all things work together for good, for those who are called according to his purpose."[2] Mine is the story of how God took a shy, insecure teenager on an overwhelming journey to strengthen his faith and teach him how to lead. The journey twists and turns and has highs and lows, discouragement and blessings, and ordinary events. My purpose in telling it is to help you develop hope and confidence in God's steadfast love for you!

CHAPTER SIX

ORIENTATION

I was a four-pound premature baby eager to get on with life, and people tell me I'm still in a hurry and over-focused. My parents were both strong Christians, and I was number three out of four brothers. Psychologists say a number-three child is often quiet. One of my former babysitters, who often took care of all four of us boys, recently tried to convince me there were only three brothers and I didn't exist, but by being "invisible" I had a lot of time to do as I pleased.

Attending school was not high on my list of exciting activities, however. I found it boring, and my report cards usually said *Jimmy isn't working to his full ability.*

THEN, OF COURSE, I WAS A TEENAGER

As the years went on, I won a few academic awards. Unfortunately, though, I had no idea what career I wanted to pursue when I graduated from high school. Remember, while my church told me "religious" service was the only occupational choice God would bless, I was counting the number of ceiling tiles. And then my dad said higher education was on me if I wasn't going into the ministry.

Aptitude tests had showed that almost any career was possible, but, as I said earlier, mechanical engineering was at the bottom of the list. I was okay with this because I viewed that field as nerdy and boring at best. But guess what. God has a sense of humor. After pursuing chemistry, math, economics, and architecture, I finally graduated from the University of Michigan with a Bachelor of Science in mechanical engineering—nine years after high school. God indeed uses His wonders to perform unexpected outcomes.

Looking back, I see how God was looking to my future even as I considered school ho-hum. One evening when I was in junior high, my mother and I were washing supper dishes when I blurted "School is unfair." When she asked why I thought so, I explained, "Only the boys with abysmal grades are released to take machine shop at Ottawa Hills High School, and I'd love to go."

My parents discussed the possibility of my taking shop class. My mother was reluctant. My dad, however, the head of the science department at a local Christian college, explained that high school science classes cover the same material I'd get in junior high only in more detail. If I took shop classes, I would not be behind in my academic subjects.

They intervened with the school, and I was able to take the machine shop class, which I continued to do all through high school. The opportunity to take those classes was a defining moment for me. It gave me new abilities, relationships, and insights I probably wouldn't have otherwise.

What I had acquired helped me later relate to coworkers, who were responsible for turning my concepts into reality, and simultaneously helped me improve my ability to create new products.

Now on to the orientation part of my leadership journey. Notice the defining moments along the way. Also notice that orientation isn't free from struggles. In fact, sometimes it can feel like disorientation is sprinkled in. But again, God is always there.

THE GARDEN EXPRESS

My vocational orientation began in 1959 when, between my first and second year of college, I started a summer business in my home state of Michigan.

The previous summer, I'd been sitting on the back porch of a neighboring Gun Lake cottage, listening to two older neighbors, Art and Jack, talk about making money. Art said, "Jim, you should start a produce route around the lake. I did it when I was in college, and I made enough money to pay my tuition with pocket money left over."

I thought it was a great way to pay my way through college. The next summer I started the Garden Express, my first real business. I leased a truck from my brother George, who ran the Volkswagen dealership in Grand Rapids, and built a wooden rack to hold the produce in the back of the truck.

You'll recall that, during high school, I'd worked at Bernie's grocery store, where Bernie gave me the responsibility of managing the produce department. So I had some experience with ordering and selling produce. That summer, I had a daily routine: get up before dawn to buy fresh produce and ice, arrange the produce into an attractive display, then drive around Gun Lake ringing my bell to attract people to buy my produce. In the evening, the process was reversed: break down the display, box up the produce, and haul it into the cooler at Besteman's Produce Co.

But I had a problem. Ten years had intervened between the time Art ran his route and I started mine. By then, most of the cottage owners had abandoned iceboxes and installed electric refrigerators, and families bought their produce in town before moving to the lake for the week. My dad was patient for a month and then approached me.

"Jim," he said, "you're working long hours and sticking to it, but I suspect you're just breaking even at best."

He was right, and he went on. "You need to find a new job, or you won't have enough money for college in the fall. Today, I was talking to Julius, one of my former students, who owns the Imperial Furniture Company. When I told him about your predicament, he said, 'It sounds like Jim is self-motivated. I can make a job available for him. Have him call Tom DeVries, my personnel manager, and he'll get him started.'" (Lots of people in Western Michigan have the name DeVries!)

I called Tom, and I was in and out of business in four weeks. The Garden Express was belly up. The failure of the company turned out to be another one of those early defining moments—painful, of course! I was crushed and embarrassed, a business failure at eighteen. However, God had a purpose in mind for me, and He would use this defining moment in multiple ways over the next years as He continued to guide me day by day.

LOVE AND MARRIAGE

Later, my life was drastically improved when my best friend, Jim Fles, said, "Did you know Judy Dykema is interested in going out with you?" I didn't realize she was, but that question motivated me to ask her to an evening hymn sing on Palm Sunday, and she said yes.

Then things got complicated because I messed up big time! That same Sunday, Nancy, a girl I'd been dating up until a month before, asked to see me, and we agreed to start dating each other again. However, I kept my date with Judy that evening, and we had a great time.

Back in school on Monday, one of Judy's friends told her I was going steady with Nancy again. Judy was disappointed, because she'd had a great time as well.

Jim Fles asked me how the date with Judy went. I said, "If I ever ask her out again, I'll marry her for sure." On the next date with Nancy, we broke up once more, this time permanently. In July, I called Judy's home to ask her if we could go out again. Her mother informed me she was on a graduation trip to Denver. I attempted to contact her repeatedly until we finally connected in mid-August, much to her mother's disgust. We went out, and this time it was love for us both.

Judy was studying to be a nurse and graduated in the spring of 1960. Both of us at the ripe old age of twenty, were married on September 5, 1961, and moved to Ann Arbor so I could study architecture, now my vocational "dream," at the University of Michigan. Calling this a defining moment would be an understatement. It was a climactic moment. The Lord had uniquely prepared Judy to help me stay the course as she accompanied me through multiple career changes over the coming years.

The Lord also blessed us with three children—David, Lynda, and Philip. Now we have nine grandchildren and two great-granddaughters! And we're still deeply in love fifty-nine years later.

SARNS, INC.

The cycle of orientation that started our journey together continued in Ann Arbor. During the winter break of our first year at the U of M, I saw a help wanted advertisement in the *Ann Arbor News*: *Part-time help wanted to buff surgical instruments . . . Call for an interview.* I called, and there was an opening for an interview at one o'clock. Little did I know this would become a gigantic defining moment in our lives. I changed into a white shirt and dress pants, hopped on my bike, and pedaled there. (We couldn't afford a car.)

I rang the doorbell, and Dick Sarns came to the door. He explained he'd started a business a few months previously, building equipment for open-heart surgery—a new medical procedure in 1961.

Dick had a small staff: two full-time machinists, a part-time draftsperson, and a few part-time employees. The company was operating out of his basement.

Dick said he was looking for someone to buff—polish—the surgical instruments and some of the other components for the heart-lung machine they were making for a cardiovascular surgeon who had just graduated from the University of Michigan medical school. I explained I'd worked my way through the first two years of college buffing hardware for furniture. (Remember, the defining moment caused by my having to close the Garden Express created that opportunity.)

He offered me the job and asked when I was available to start. I replied, "I rode my bike over and might as well start right now." He looked strangely at me because it's a dirty job and I had on a white shirt.

As I went to work that afternoon, two of his employees, Larry and Peter, made it clear they thought I was severely short in the brain department. Maybe that's one reason I didn't realize this position was a gigantic defining moment for Judy and me. While I was still intent on becoming an architect, God was using this job to support us and train me for future opportunities in various ways.

BLESSINGS

That spring, Judy and I needed to find a larger place because a baby was on the way. Working on an hourly basis, I was worried about affording to rent a house and pay expenses; hospital rules at the time prevented Judy from working at the hospital while pregnant. We didn't have health insurance, and I didn't see a way to pay for the upcoming medical expenses. Despite God's provision, I thought I was responsible for our care, not God.

A month later, this advertisement appeared in the *Ann Arbor News: House for rent to a Christian couple.* (Such a restriction was still allowed in the 1960s.) I called, and the owner, who now lived in the Detroit area, explained that the previous renters had moved out in mid-winter and the place was trashed and in bad shape. He told me where to find a key so I could look inside.

He was right. The house was a dump. However, after shop classes and two years of architectural schooling, I believed it could be fixed up to make it livable, so I called him back.

We were paying $90 a month for a one-bedroom apartment, and he wanted $95 a month for this three-bedroom house. Also, any money I spent on repairs would be deducted from the rent, and the rent wouldn't start until we moved in, which meant no double payments. If I wanted to do additional repairs, all I had to do was give him an estimate, and he would send the money.

I took Judy to see it. She was less than excited, but she was willing to go ahead. We cleaned up the house the best we could and turned one bedroom into a lovely nursery. Our parents were also less than happy when they saw the place, but God answered our prayers to bless that house and our family while we lived there for the next four years. God also worked all things out by providing an almost-new car.

As it turned out, the U of M Hospital bill for Judy's prenatal care, delivery, and stay was only $5 because I was a student, and by the time David was born, I was on salary at Sarns, Inc., which included health insurance for the family. God was clearly showing me He had supplied and would continue to supply our family's needs.

DREAMS COME TRUE

Sarns, Inc., grew, and a few months later it moved into a small manufacturing building on the outskirts of Ann Arbor. Meanwhile, Dick had promoted me from the buffing room to the drafting board at Larry and Pete's request. I began doing some engineering design work, which involved coming up with designs for some bizarre requests from researchers at the University of Michigan.

One project was an automated IV pump that could measure a future mother's labor contractions and control the drug infusion rate during the induction of labor. At the other end of the spectrum, the dental school had me design a machine to test the wear on toothbrushes.

Architecture school was fascinating, but the summer after my first semester, a slump occurred in the construction industry. Only one graduating senior in the U of M School of Architecture found work as an architect. At the same time, God continued to supply our family's needs marvelously. I was now working full-time, and Dick was paying me a salary equivalent to a starting graduate engineer.

Dr. Gordon Van Wylen, the dean of the engineering school at the U of M, attended the same church Judy and I did, and Judy often babysat for his children. He knew I was working for Sarns along with being an architectural student. One Sunday morning, he pulled me aside and said, "Jim, the mechanical engineering department is planning to begin a major in bioengineering. Would you be interested in switching your major to mechanical engineering? I think we can transfer most of your credits in architecture to equivalent mechanical engineering courses."

God certainly does have a sense of humor. Remember, my test scores in high school showed my lowest aptitude was in mechanical engineering. But under the circumstances, this was an answer to prayer, and I jumped at the opportunity. This was another defining moment for us as well as one of God's wonders.

Sarns, Inc., continued to grow. Eventually, I was responsible for product development, quality control, and what would today be called IT. I had learned to program the IBM computer that had 4K of memory in assembly language and developed a complete inventory control system. That system enabled the company to rapidly respond to changes.

I helped develop new heart-lung machines—including the one used for the first heart transplant in South Africa—and kidney dialysis and peritoneal dialysis machines to treat kidney failure. The company continued to grow rapidly. Dick paid me generously, and at age thirty, I reached the salary level I'd set as my life goal.

Working at Sarns was a dream come true. I had always been interested in medicine; however, every time I thought about pursuing it as a career, all I could remember was fainting when I cut myself and saw what seemed like all my blood oozing over the floor. So what had the Lord arranged? He put me in an operating room with a heart-lung machine pumping about twelve liters of blood around and doctors opening the patient's chest and stopping the heart to repair it, both of which were guaranteed to make the faint in heart queasy.

God's sense of humor was working again. Indeed, this was a career or "calling" I had never envisioned for myself or ever would have attempted on my own initiative!

A LESSON IN LEADERSHIP

However, everything was not smooth sailing for Sarns, Inc. We'd developed a kidney dialysis machine and blood pump for Baxter Laboratories in Morton Grove, Illinois, and these and their associated products were now a significant part of Sarns, Inc's sales. Then Baxter suddenly announced, on terse notice, that it had purchased a manufacturing company in Silver Spring, Maryland, and they planned to move the production of the dialysis products from Sarns to the new company.

The kidney dialysis product line represented a significant portion of Sarns, Inc's business, and Dick needed to decide whether to lay off people. Instead, he made a courageous decision to expand. He borrowed money and purchased an extensive amount of equipment to enable us to make all the sheet metal cabinets for our other products instead of using a variety of vendors. His decision to protect "his people" rather than reducing the workforce was a living example of his integrity. It was a vital lesson on the right way to care for those who depended on me when I was later in charge of my own business.

SPIRITUAL GROWTH

Judy and I had been living "protected" lives as young Christians, and we were comfortable in our Christian tradition. But then I was serving on the local Youth for Christ board composed of Christians from different traditions than ours, and we found some of their actions unusual from our perspective.

For example, they routinely called and prayed with us over the phone. In our tradition, we only ever heard the pastor or an elder pray out loud, much less expected God to hear "phone" prayers. God was gently expanding our horizons.

Then Judy and I attended a seminar called Basic Youth Conflicts with others from our church. At the workshop, they challenged me to reevaluate my priorities. I was a workaholic, and I came to realize I needed to reorder my life and make serving God and my family my top priorities. After the seminar, I wrote out a list of "new" priorities and pasted them on the mirror in my bathroom. Although some mornings I was tempted to shave with my eyes closed, they helped me stay on the new course. Attending this seminar became a significant defining moment.

I continued part-time with my studies at the University of Michigan School of Engineering and worked more than full-time at Sarns, Inc. I was a deacon at and the treasurer of our local church, and I was president of the local Youth for Christ chapter. As time passed, Judy and I felt the time we spent working with YFC was rewarding when we saw hearts changed spiritually, not just physically repaired.

Over the next three years, I began praying for a vocational full-time ministry opportunity. I prayed not because I believed only that type of work counted—God was using us in a variety of significant ways—but because God seemed to be calling me.

I just didn't know this was the beginning of my disorientation.

CHAPTER SEVEN

DISORIENTATION

A s a result of my prayers, God arranged for me to meet Nicky Cruz. Nicky was a former gang leader from New York City who had accepted the Lord as a result of Rev. Dave Wilkerson's ministry. Dave Wilkerson's book *The Cross and the Switchblade* and Nicky's book *Run Baby Run* tell their stories.

By this time, Nicky had both a ministry for drug-addicted young adults, Nicky Cruz Outreach, and a crusade ministry. In the fall of 1971, he was in Ann Arbor for a crusade, and I was responsible for taking him to the airport. We'd met previously on one of his trips to Ann Arbor. As Nicky was getting out of the car, he turned to me and asked, "Jim, would you be interested in serving as my executive director for the ministry?"

I paused before answering. In my mind, it was as if God was saying to me, *You've been whining about a full-time Christian service position, so either swing at the ball I've pitched or stop whining.* I told Nicky I was interested. Later that fall, I made a trip to Raleigh, North Carolina, and we discussed the details of the position, then decided to proceed. This was yet another and new defining moment.

However, once back in Ann Arbor, I was anxious about quitting my job at Sarns, Inc. I'd thought about resigning several years previously to finish the classwork needed to get my bachelor's degree in mechanical engineering. At that time, I'd talked with Dick about leaving to finish my classwork in order to graduate. He asked about how long it would take me if I attended full-time.

I talked with my advisor and determined that if I took fourteen hours in summer school, followed by four hours in the fall semester, I would graduate. Dick then offered my full salary for the summer while releasing me to attend school full-time.

Because of Dick's kindness and concern for Judy and me, leaving Sarns, Inc., was not like resigning a position with a huge company where I would have been just a number. Dick was a generous friend, a tremendous mentor, and a father figure, not only an employer.

The night before I was to resign, I came across this passage in my Bible:

> Jesus said, "Truly, I say to you, there is no one who has left house or brothers or sisters or mother or father or children or lands, for my sake and for the gospel, who will not receive a hundredfold now in this time, houses and brothers and sisters and mothers and children and lands, with persecutions, and in the age to come eternal life."[1]

These verses gave me the courage to talk with Dick the next day and explain why I was making such a drastic decision.

God worked countless wonders to get us moved from Ann Arbor to Raleigh. The day after I resigned, Dick called me into his office and gave me a check for several months' salary to "tide" us over. But we still had a house to sell and a home to buy, and we had to arrange for our move from Michigan to North Carolina. We also needed to learn how to live on one third of my current salary and get children settled in a new school.

God performed many wonders, even though we had several precarious points in the process. He stretched and grew our faith by leaps and bounds. This chapter would be longer than a book if I were to list everything God orchestrated to provide us with an orderly move and protect our family.

LEARNING A NEW JOB—JUST NOT THE ONE I EXPECTED

Once in Raleigh, I started my new job on the following Monday. LaRue, the office manager responsible for writing payroll checks, came into my office and closed the door. She said, "Jim, I thought you ought to know we don't have any money to make Friday's payroll, and I don't know where the money will come from."

My due diligence when visiting Raleigh before taking the position had been "emotional," but I knew the ministry was stressed. Yet this was certainly not what I'd anticipated. God was going to teach me about praying under fire, and He answered those prayers. He was faithful in supplying funds not only to meet that payroll but also every one of the payrolls during my stay. The funds were always available exactly when needed.

God taught me this lesson over and over again: He seldom gives us all the money we need or think we need upfront. He wants us to take the first step in faith alone.

A few weeks later, I was sitting in the hallway outside a room where Nicky's board of directors was meeting. Nicky was away on a crusade. Dan, the only board member I'd met, came out and asked me to join them. After Dan introduced me, Mark, an upset board chairman, addressed me: "The organization is bankrupt. We're meeting today to begin the process of closing down. We never authorized Nicky to hire you!"

How could I reply to that? But God guided me. I was able to relate my board experience at YFC, my responsibilities at Sarns, Inc., and the precarious position their decision would create for my family. Mark then asked me to join them in prayer for wisdom and guidance. God used this time of prayer to change their minds, and they gave me the time to put the ministry back in order with God's help.

Yet because of the disorientation of leaving a steady job, moving my family to an unfamiliar state, and finding an organization in chaos, I then experienced a "valley of death" experience, triggered by a minor incident.

I had gone to the lumberyard so I could buy boards to build bookshelves in our new family room. In Michigan, I could buy white pine boards, which have a beautiful grain and are often free of knots. In North Carolina, all I could find was yellow pine, full of knots and sap, a terrible disappointment for a craftsman.

On the way home, I had to pull over to the side of the road because I couldn't see through my tears. But God remains faithful, and to this day He uses the memory of His provision in Raleigh to encourage me when I encounter a difficult time. He does work all things for good.

MOVING FORWARD DESPITE CHALLENGES

God taught me how to pray for Nicky Cruz Outreach. He also taught me how to pray for my family's well-being, and He continued with His wonders.

Let me share one small example of His care. At the church we attended in Raleigh, Judy and I were teaching the youth group, and we were planning to take them on a retreat into the mountains for the coming weekend. Unfortunately, I didn't have suitable clothes to wear, and we didn't have the money to buy them.

Then the Wednesday before we were to leave, I came home for lunch and found a check in the mail from an insurance company—a company that, to the best of my knowledge, we'd never used. It was exactly enough money to purchase the necessary clothes.

Judy, our children, and I agree that our time with Nicky was not only fulfilling but at times exciting. For example, our daughter, Lynda, sat on *Andraé* Crouch's lap as he played "Soon and Very Soon" for the first time in private.

I had the opportunity to work on producing a film called *Satan on the Loose*, which opened my eyes to the spiritual warfare around us. We even interviewed a former witch and warlock in our living room. They told us stories about the frightening experiences they had while involved in the occult.

We also joined a wonderful teaching church and had the opportunity to be taught in a small group Bible study by a student of Watchman Nee.

I'd never been involved in an organization's finances except for being treasurer at church. At Sarns, Inc., my only involvement was cashing my check. But I found my responsibilities at Nicky Cruz Outreach were primarily closing the non-functional parts of the ministry and building new budgets and control systems. The former executive director had left with the list of contributors, and the operating system needed to support the record-keeping and mailing involved. This crippled the organization's fund-raising ability, and all the donor-base records needed to be recovered.

The Lord blessed abundantly, and after two years, it was apparent I had completed the tasks God had asked of me as executive director. He'd added knowledge about finance and budgets to the training He'd already given me, and He used my stay with Nicky to train me in areas of leadership, where I lacked knowledge or experience. With its reduced size, the ministry no longer needed an executive director. Nicky and I discussed the situation, and as friends, we agreed it was time for me to search for a new job.

THE CHALLENGE OF CHANGE

Disorientation continued relentlessly. Called to be in ministry and now about to be unemployed, I struggled with many questions. Had God called me to work permanently in a full-time vocational ministry? Did He find me wanting in some way? How would my family be provided for in the transition (because by that time our savings were nonexistent)? Should I be looking for a position with another ministry purely because of my vocational guilt? Or did God have something new in mind for us as a family?

One noon I was sitting in a shopping mall near the office, watching an artist build a gigantic sandcastle. The sculpture seemed symbolic of my life as it crumbled before my eyes. While sitting there, a man sat down next to me and said, "You look deep in thought and troubled. Do you mind sharing with me?"

My personality is high on the quiet and private side; however, counter to my norm, I spent the better part of the next hour sharing my story with him. His response? "The Lord doesn't always call a person to a single occupation for their entire lifetime. Perhaps He's used this to prepare you for something new He has in store."

I never saw that man again, but I know the Lord sent him. This verse came to my mind as he left: "Let brotherly love continue. Do not neglect to show hospitality to strangers, for thereby some have entertained angels unawares."[2] I wondered if perhaps he was an angel.

God used the job changes, the stress on Judy and me and our family, and His great answers to prayer to refine us and bring us closer to each other and Him. In the short time I'd been with Nicky, God gave me the equivalent of a master's degree in finance, new communication skills, a new appreciation for people struggling with addictions, and new friends. He deepened my understanding of the spiritual realm and the struggles surrounding us as a result. He demonstrated His care and love for us as He walked beside us in both good times and challenging times.

I would without doubt call the years I spent with Nicky more than a defining moment; they were more like a refiner's fire. Yet my family and I look back at those years as happy, exciting times.

JOB SEARCH

I really did need to search for a new job, because there would be no more income in six weeks. I first contacted Dick Sarns, and his reaction was one of surprise. "Let me think about it, and I'll call you back in two weeks," he said. When he did, his answer was, "Jim, I'd love to have you back. However, long term, I don't think you'd remain happy if you weren't the company president, and I still like being president."

He was right, and as a result, we remain close friends fifty years later.

My next call was to Pete, now a senior vice president at Baxter Laboratories. I'd worked with him and other senior Baxter managers while developing a modular heart-lung machine and various types of dialysis equipment for them. I had designed profitable products for them, developed under impossibly tight schedules.

When I asked if he had a place for me in one of his divisions, his immediate reply was, "Yes, Jim, my divisions have several ongoing projects that need the kind of help you can provide. Your base location will be in our research facility in Round Lake, Illinois. Let me talk with my division presidents, and we'll choose a project. Then you can come to Illinois to interview as a formality. You have a job if you want one."

Did I want one? This was an answer to prayer. I had a new job at more than my former salary at Sarns, starting before my last day with Nicky Cruz Outreach.

NEW JOB, NEW JOBS

However, disorientation continued. At Thanksgiving time, I moved alone to Illinois. The family needed to stay in Raleigh until school was over and we sold our house. We were thankful for the new job, but it was an immense strain on both Judy and me and our family to be living apart. And it got worse. Before we were settled as a family once again, we would experience three more moves, three new school systems, and many lonely times over a two-year period. I had a new job that absorbed my attention plus, but Judy had three children to guide through a stressful time.

At Baxter, the project I was assigned was to assist with redesigning a dialysis machine they'd acquired from another company. The device was unique and used technology beyond the other products on the market. Because of its complexity, neither Baxter nor the company they'd purchased it from had successfully manufactured one of the machines. The failure rate on the production line was so high they were never able to get even a single unit to pass final quality control.

My responsibility was to transfer information from the team of design engineers doing the redesign in Illinois to the production team in Silver Spring, Maryland, and help supervise the production. Time was running out. The goal given was to ship at least one dialysis machine to a customer in time to qualify it under the grandfather clause in the upcoming FDA medical device regulations.

As the engineers redesigned the various subsystems in Illinois, we had to order new parts and return unused parts. Using my experience from Sarns, I developed a rudimentary requirement planning system for the Silver Spring facility to ensure the components would be obtained on time to meet the expedited schedule. I added a requirement that all electronic parts be run for at least one hundred hours by the manufacturer before shipping to us to minimize the premature failure of the electronics. By doing this, we eliminated the early losses that had kept the devices from passing final quality control.

The team made it, and we shipped the first machine the day before the grandfather clause took effect.

A few weeks later, I received another call from Pete with a new job offer. Was his call because I was trying to be the best Christ-centered leader I knew how to be? In part, but I don't think that was the only reason. Pete wasn't interested in my ability to be a Christ-centered leader. However, he appreciated the way it helped me bridge across different interest groups and unite them together in a common goal. Based on my history of leadership performance and because of my dedication to achieving the goals of the job at hand, he was confident I would successfully lead a team to reach the objective.

Again God was preparing me for future assignments. As leaders, we can act ethically, show concern, be a servant, and appear spiritual. Still, if we've developed a reputation for poor performance, we can't be effective in being a reflection of Christ. His objective while on earth was to train His followers to lead well, and then He trusted them to reach their objective—to make disciples.[3]

Pete was calling because another one of his divisions had a stalled project and needed a prototype for the upcoming blood bank meeting the next spring, less than ten months away. This project was in the concept stage and had some enormous technical problems to overcome. Also, two design groups were involved with competing ideas, and no one had the authority to determine the project's direction. One team was in Round Lake and the other in Silver Spring.

Pete asked me to interview with the Director of Development for the Fenwal division, also based in Round Lake. I did, and the director requested that I be transferred from the artificial organ's division to his development group to lead the project.

The project was to develop a centrifuge to harvest matched white cells to treat leukemia in children and, if technically feasible, a person's stem cells for bone marrow transplant procedures for treating lymphoma. The plastic tubes carrying blood into and out of the centrifuge could not have a rotating seal. This was necessary to ensure the harvested cells would meet storage requirements dictated by blood-banking rules. A rotating seal could expose the blood to air, which would prevent it from being stored and then reinfused, because to do so violated blood-banking regulations.

Can you imagine running multiple tubes into and out of a centrifuge running at 1,000+ RPM without anything tangling up? The Round Lake design team had found a solution they called "one omega two omega." I spent hours at the kitchen table with a piece of string before I figured out how it worked.

The development of the product, however, was only part of the problem facing me. The two design groups had different cultures, and there was a lack of respect by both teams for the other group's concepts. Guiding the project meant I was on a shuttle schedule. Chicago was my base, but I spent every other week in Silver Spring. Once everyone understood how they contributed to the success of the project and we developed a plan, the level of trust grew between the two teams.

The project was just beginning to come together when I received another call from Pete. They'd just fired the senior management of a small medical device company Baxter had recently purchased. It made IV catheters in Dallas, Texas. Pete informed me I was to serve as the acting development manager to help solve some problems until they found new management. This responsibility was in addition to my current responsibilities. Now the travel circuit was increased—Chicago, then Silver Spring, on to Dallas, and then back to Chicago.

Pete finished the call by adding the comment, "This new assignment doesn't let you off the hook from having a working prototype of the pheresis system so we can show it at the blood-banking convention in Atlanta."

The team worked well together and successfully delivered an innovative pheresis system by the target date Pete set.

A RECKONING

My family had finally moved from Raleigh to Libertyville, Illinois, but only for a brief stop in a rental condo and a new school system. We would eventually purchase a house in McHenry, thirty miles from Libertyville.

Judy and the children were exhausted. The children had now been in three school systems within two years, and they knew there would be a fourth at the end of that school year. Judy had moved two times cross-country, and now, for all practical purposes, she had an absentee husband. Not at all our desire for the way to raise a family.

When we (well, Judy) completed the move to McHenry, and the heightened travel continued, Judy had had enough. When I returned home one Friday night from an extended trip, she met me at the door and said, "This travel has to come to an end. You come home for the weekend and disrupt the family routine when the kids and I have just become comfortable. Quite frankly, sometimes I think it would be easier if you just stayed away."

She was right. I would leave on Sunday afternoon for a week or more, allowing just enough time for her to get the kids settled back into a routine, and then I would come home and mess everything up. She asked if I could do anything to cut down on travel.

I found an opening in another of Pete's divisions, Medical Products, and applied for the director of development position. At the interview, the president of that division said the job was mine and asked when I could start. This was an answer to our prayers. The promotion meant minimal travel and no move required.

But before I could make the transfer, Pete called Ron Williams, the director of development for the Fenwal division, to whom I reported. Pete directed Ron to tell me the chairman of the board of Baxter Laboratories, William (Bill) Graham, had blocked the transfer. The chairman's explanation was this: "The projects Jim is leading, most of them dealing with a possible cure for or treatment of cancer, are more critical to Baxter's success than the whole Medical Products division."

I explained to Ron that I was looking at the transfer as a way to substantially reduce travel for family reasons. After some discussion, I received a promise from Dale Smith, the Fenwal division president, who reported to Pete and told me the travel problem would be taken care of within six months. Meanwhile, I would have the same pay grade as a director of development position.

Six months passed, disorientation continued, and both Dale and Pete had resigned and left the company. Travel was even worse. Judy and I considered our options and found only two—for me to quit and find another job or for us to start our own company.

Neither choice sounded particularly attractive to us. I had tried my own business while in college (remember the Garden Express), and it had been a failure. And having worked at Sarns, Inc., while it was a small developing company, I knew the momentous commitment starting and running a small business required. Also, despite my earlier intentions, I was still a certified workaholic.

After Judy and I prayed and talked about it for several weeks, we concluded starting our own company was most likely the right option.

AND YET . . .

If we were to start our own company, Judy and I faced three seemingly insurmountable problems: no product idea, no money, and the fact that Baxter "owned" my brain. But nothing serious, right?

Not to God. He'd been working out His plan, and He saw only "good" from His perspective.

I had experience building hardware but minimal experience in the design and manufacturing of sterile disposable products. But then Baxter had provided me with in-depth expertise in making complicated disposables, and at the IV company, I had gained experience in building high-volume, simpler sterile devices. God had guided all these events and given me what amounted to a medical degree in designing and making sterile disposable products.

Before we continue the story, let me share five things God taught me through these various experiences, opportunities, and challenges.

1. Every person is equally valuable in God's eyes, and I needed to consistently model that as a leader, totally and completely.
2. Making me responsible for an impossibly complex development project in a pressure-cooker environment was how God chose to force me to learn how to delegate to and empower a team.
3. God walks before me to clear the way, particularly when I don't feel Him or see Him and feel abandoned and trapped in circumstances of my own making.
4. God always makes a successful way through a problem, a lesson that was repeatedly reinforced and helped me move forward in faith countless times, as you will see as my story continues.
5. People at all levels surrounding me learn much more from my actions than from my speech.

God had been writing my life story, leading me to the point where I would be able to pursue the opportunity to start our own company.

Let's review the path God had taken my life up to this point.

1. While in Ann Arbor, I eventually received an engineering degree, giving me formal accreditation.

2. Judy and I attended a seminar called Basic Youth Conflicts. During that week, I made a new list of personal priorities and committed them to the Lord, helping me keep my life in proper balance. I frequently lost the way, but He always pushed me back into balance even when I was unwilling.

3. At Sarns, Inc., I learned about the process of design and fabrication of a new product and turning a concept into a successful business. And by observation, I learned how to start an entrepreneurial company as well. My stay there provided me with experience in every area of a company except for finance. And even more important, I had a mentor who taught me that following a moral path was necessary to real success and that people are important.

4. At Nicky Cruz Outreach, God gave me nearly the equivalent of an MBA in finance.

5. While working at Sarns, Inc., I had learned about building machines, but I knew only a little about making disposable sterile devices. At Baxter Laboratories, I needed that hardware experience, and I acquired the necessary skills and training to manufacture sterile disposable products. The size and scope of their projects forced me to grow as a leader, and as a result I learned how to delegate as well as how to be a more effective leader. Along the way, God had also given me a variety of other leadership skills.

God had been preparing Judy and me to start a new medical device business. But from our viewpoint, it was impossible. We faced those three roadblocks: no product idea, no money, and the fact that Baxter "owned" my brain. We questioned if this was a "three strikes and you're out" situation. But God knew what He was doing.

CHAPTER EIGHT

REORIENTATION

This is how God started my reorientation period.

First, he solved the "no product" roadblock by putting me back in touch with John, a surgical assistant I'd worked with on several development projects. When I asked if he had any problems I could help solve, he mentioned a new medical technique called cardioplegia delivery that was just beginning to come to the attention of heart surgeons.

At that time, the heart was the only major organ not well protected during surgery. When the surgeon planned out the steps for the surgery, he or she needed to provide periodic time intervals so the surgery could be interrupted to allow blood to perfuse the heart, preventing damage to it at a cellular level because of the lack of oxygen. This new technique protected the heart, and, for the first time, allowed surgery to proceed without interruption, significantly decreasing the time a patient needed to be on bypass.

This technique was a substantial improvement in protection for the heart, enabled the length of the surgery to be decreased, and made more complex procedures possible.

All are significant improvements for the patient. Patients come off bypass sooner and with healthier hearts.

John told me he needed a small disposable connector that wasn't commercially available to deliver the cardioplegia effectively. He had offered the idea to Sarns, but they weren't interested, opening the way for me to have a product that didn't compete with their product line. I didn't want to interfere with Dick's business because of the gracious way he'd treated me.

I arranged to see John and watch an operation using cardioplegia in his laboratory. After observing the operation, I suggested a design for a catheter that would eliminate the need for the connector. Also, it would make the whole procedure even simpler and faster. I went home and made a prototype using parts from a hemodialysis catheter and an IV catheter from my desk drawer. An accident? I don't think so. Remember the dialysis and IV catheter experience God had given me.

I took it back to John, and we used it in his laboratory with outstanding results. We now had the concept for a new product, and the first roadblock—no product—was gone.

MONEY, MONEY

The next roadblock was no money. How would God supply the necessary funds? Judy and I continued to pray, and I developed a five-year operating and financial plan. The prime interest rate at the time was 11.75 percent. We had no indication it would be at its all-time high of 21.5 percent by the end of our first year of operation, making obtaining a loan close to impossible.

Mr. Hugh Cummings from Burlington, North Carolina, had become a friend and mentor while I was with Nicky Cruz. Every time I'd met with him, he'd encouraged me with at least one story about a wondrous intervention of God he'd experienced. I sent my business plan to him to get his input as a seasoned businessman.

Hugh called me. "Jim, why don't you come to Burlington so we can visit face-to-face?" I did, and after we caught up with our lives, he said, "I've studied your plan. I have confidence you can do it, and I'm excited. Would you consider me as an investor?'

Of course, my answer was yes. After we agreed on a price for 33 percent of the company's stock, he asked, "Where are you going to get the funding for your half of the company?"

"I don't know. Perhaps a second mortgage on my house."

"After your time with Nicky, I'm sure there's no way you can have that amount of equity. In fact, you're most likely still close to being broke. Can I lend you the money you need for your share?"

In my wildest imagination, I couldn't have dreamed up a scenario like this. I went back to Chicago, and when I went to work the next day, Ron Williams, to whom I reported, called me into his office to hear how the visit went. He was well aware of my frustration over the blocked transfer and extensive travel, and I had told him I was thinking about starting a business. Ron asked me how the trip went, and our conversation went like this:

"Mr. Cummings wants 33 percent of the stock; so I only have to find someone to purchase the remaining 16 percent to move ahead."

Ron asked, "If I can sell my Corvette, can I purchase the remaining 16 percent?"

Only someone who's tried to raise the capital to start a business can understand what a miracle this was. In one week, God had supplied enough money so we could begin. No mass mailings, no scrambling for contacts, no banks, and no venture capitalists. Talk about God doing wonders.

A few years later, I heard a venture capitalist talk, and from his comments I realized that raising this amount of money in such a short period was an impossibility. Even if it were possible, the cost would be surrendering the control of the company to a venture capital firm. But God had supplied enough resources, and roadblock number two was gone.

GIVE ME BACK MY BRAIN

Roadblock number three was that Baxter owned my brain. When I explained my plan to Bob, the new Fenwal president, and explained why I wanted to pursue starting my own company, he replied, "Let me talk with the new senior vice president, and I'll get back with you."

He did and then came back with a proposal. Baxter was offering an unconditional release from my non-compete agreement for the cardiovascular surgery area and also to pay my full salary if I would continue working for them and transition incrementally over the next ninety days. In a large corporation like Baxter, this kind of offer is nearly impossible, another marvelous wonder. Roadblock number three was gone too!

Bob asked if he could help and if I would share my business plan with him. He studied the project and offered me this opinion: "You're severely undercapitalized." Was I fearful? Yes. Did I believe God was encouraging Judy and me to step forward in faith? Yes. But I also believed God wanted us to remember this verse: "We know that for those who love God all things work together for good, for those who are called according to his purpose."[1]

DLP, INC.

Judy and I chose DLP, Inc., for the company's name. The three letters came from the first letter of each of our children's names—David, Lynda, and Philip. We thought it fit since they were the motivating force behind our desire to start a company. We incorporated in February 1979, completed development of our first product, tested it, obtained FDA approval, had the necessary injection molds made, and filled the orders we had received, one of which was to an international distributor in Japan seven months later in August 1979. And we made a profit for that month and our first fiscal year. Another great set of wonders.

DLP's size increased over the succeeding years. In 1980 we outgrew the dentist's office we'd rented in McHenry and moved to a school building we remodeled in Grand Rapids, Michigan, Judy's and my hometown.

In September 1981, I read a fascinating book by Keith Miller, *The Taste of New Wine*.[2] He was a businessman who worked for an oil company in Austin, Texas. I had never read a book like it.

Keith was transparent about both his business and his personal life. He was open and honest about his struggles in all areas and so brutally honest that I instantly related to his struggles. He made no distinctions between how he acted between work, home, and church. He didn't attempt to cover his warts, bruises, and outright failures to live as he thought God would want him to live. He was an authentic leader.

Keith talked about how honesty and openness can revolutionize our relationship with God and others. He accurately pointed out that the biggest obstacle to relationships was our unwillingness to acknowledge our brokenness and imperfections.

He also talked about his struggles between his outward piety and his inward love of self. The many examples he gave in the book made it come alive to me. It completely changed my view on how God wanted me to live out my life in the world. While writing this book, I discovered *The Taste of New Wine* was listed among the one hundred Christian books that changed the twentieth century, according to authors William and Randy Petersen.[3]

In 1983, Ron Williams left Baxter Laboratories and brought his family to Grand Rapids to become the president of DLP, Inc. By 1983 we had outgrown our facility and moved into a remodeled factory. The new factory provided us the manufacturing and office space we needed because of our growing product line.

STUMBLING BLOCK

Not everything was smooth sailing. In fall 1984, Judy and I were sitting before a federal magistrate in Kalamazoo. Another small company, for whom we'd been helping market their products, had sued us for patent infringement. They claimed one of our minor products, called a coronary cannula, infringed on their patent for a similar device. According to our patent attorney, there was no possibility of an infringement. The purpose of the meeting with the magistrate was to urge us to settle the suit rather than take up the court's time.

We thought the legal system was interested in justice—who was right and who was wrong. But after listening to us, the magistrate said, "I'm setting another interview in four weeks. Since this case is just about money, I expect you to have settled with the other firm by that time so I can take this case off the court's calendar." Judy and I looked at each other, both of us in total shock. What happened to justice?

I had several discussions with the president of the other company, but he refused to budge from his position because this was his only product. I have a high-control type of personality, and I had little if any control over this situation. That meant God needed to give me another defining moment, which came only after I'd fought this lawsuit for several months.

About four months after the last meeting with the magistrate, I attended a convention of the American Society of Thoracic Surgeons to display our product line and meet with cardiovascular surgeons. During a slow time in the exhibit area, I wandered around looking at other exhibits. I stopped to talk with a friend who was displaying his products—reusable cannulas. He had an unusual cannula on his exhibit table. I asked him what kind of cannula it was, and he told me it was a coronary cannula.

I looked at it closer and realized it worked the same way the cannula made by the opposing companies did. I asked him what year he'd made it, and he told me about ten years earlier. He also said the design was obsolete, but he kept trying to sell it. When I asked how much he wanted for the cannula, he told me $65. I gladly paid him for it and brought it back to Grand Rapids with me.

When you apply for a patent, you must disclose any product you know exists that is the same or similar to your idea. Of course, if both products are the same and the other one existed before you invented yours, you'll be denied a patent. When I returned, I called the president of the company suing us and asked for a face-to-face meeting with no attorneys present. He asked if his major investor could be present, which I encouraged.

The day came, and the three of us met around a conference table. I placed my newly purchased coronary cannula on the table and asked if he had ever seen it before.

"Yes," he said.

"When did you file for your patent?"

"Two years ago," he replied.

"Did you disclose this cannula to the patent office in your application?"

"No."

At this point his investor interrupted the conversation. "Would you mind if Bob and I go out in the hall to talk for a few minutes?"

When they returned, the investor asked if I would be willing to just walk away and absorb my legal expenses to date if the lawsuit were withdrawn.

This experience was indeed another defining moment for me. It was as if the Lord was saying, *Jim, would you rather have justice from the courts or from Me?* It was another one of His wonders. I wish I could testify that I learned my lesson well, but as you will see later, when we talk about uncontrolled anger, I can be a slow learner.

CHAPTER NINE

DISORIENTATION AND RESOLUTION—AGAIN

G od was still "stirring up."

In late 1993 I received a puzzling call from a salesperson I'd trained at Baxter Laboratories in the late 1960s. After we talked for a while and caught up on the events of the intervening years, he said, "I'm going to be in your area next week. Could I stop by and see your place?"

I told him I'd love to talk and give him a tour. The day arrived, and he told me he was now working for a company called Medtronic, Inc., in Minneapolis. They were looking for acquisitions that complemented their cardiovascular business, and he asked if we would be open to an offer for DLP, Inc.

I expressed that we were reluctant to consider a sale based on the time involved and the results we had when in discussion with suitors in the past. However, I offered to take him on a tour of our plant and provide some simple information. We later found out they were in final negotiations for our closest competitor, and he was just verifying the competitor's claims about DLP.

Ron, who had joined us in 1983 as president, and I discussed the visit and thought the issue was dead. A few weeks later, though, Ron received a call from Dr. Glen Nelson, vice chairman of Medtronic, Inc. Dr. Nelson shared with Ron that Medtronic was very interested in talking further about acquiring DLP, Inc. After he had that conversation, Ron and I asked each other what an offer would need to be for us to consider it seriously.

We discussed several questions that needed to be answered and what our objectives would be in a sale and then wrote them down and filed them away. Ron called Dr. Nelson back to talk with him about these issues, and then Dr. Nelson asked if he and Bill George, the COO of Medtronic, could visit.

Medtronic was persistent and eventually met the terms Ron and I set. We concluded the sale by the end of March 1994. We had achieved every entrepreneur's dream—start a company with next to nothing and then sell it for a lot of money.

Ron and I also each received a four-year employment agreement as part of Medtronic's upper management. Initially, Ron reported to the COO, Art Collins, and I reported to Dr. Glenn Nelson. The employees were well taken care of as a result of the sale, and Medtronic, Inc., treated them well, but both Ron and I had personally struggled in making the transition even though the cultures of both organizations were compatible. Most of the systems and procedures we'd developed to run our business needed to be changed to mesh with Medtronic's systems. The major decisions we'd both been making for DLP now required corporate approval.

Things were changing for us on a personal basis, and I, at least, felt I had lost a big part of my identity.

Both Ron and I had also underestimated the pressure put on public companies to meet their quarterly forecasts. Individually, and at different times, we both served on Medtronic's operating committee, responsible for the strategy needed to meet the performance numbers forecasted by the stock market analysts. Even a penny difference in a public corporation's performance compared to the forecasted quarterly earnings drastically affects a company's stock prices, and this in turn affects the employees' retirement and profit-sharing accounts and continues to cascade through an organization both positively and negatively. This pressure was passed along to Ron and me as a part of senior management.

MEANWHILE...

In 1996, before I left Medtronic, three partners and I purchased the John Widdicomb Company, which made extremely high-end residential furniture. It was founded in 1858, even before the United States Civil War began. The company had been in difficulty for several years and was still in existence only because its former owner, the chairman of East Jordan Iron Works, had viewed it as a hobby before he died. His family wasn't interested in continuing to invest money in it, but I was interested in buying the company for four reasons.

1. I wanted to see if it was possible to return the company's terrible culture back to health and whether a healthy culture would make enough improvement in financial performance to make it a viable company again.
2. I was interested in furniture design and manufacturing because of my involvement in the industry during my early college years—and because of my love for design.
3. I thought I could easily afford it.
4. I thought it would be fun.

As we entered 1997, not only had I realized I'd underestimated the difficulty of turning around the operation, but my interest had waned. Owning the company was also requiring a continual infusion of large amounts of capital, and it wasn't fun. So cross out reasons 3 and 4!

I was a mental wreck, caused in part by the amount of disorientation in my life. The psychological effects of selling DLP, Inc., the financial struggles brought on by the losses at John Widdicomb, and the 1996 suicide of a pastor friend I'd been mentoring all worked together to collapse my world, which had turned into shades of gray.

I had lost all hope for the future. Everything seemed to take more energy than I had available. Simple tasks looked like mountains to climb. Fortunately, Judy lovingly confronted me and said, "I know you're miserable; however, because we love you, we're miserable as well. Promise me you'll get help. I've heard good things about Dr. Sam. Why don't you make an appointment?"

I did, and after evaluation, the doctor said, "Jim, I'm sorry, but you've entered into clinical depression." Those are dreadful words for anyone. But God used Dr. Sam's help, medication, and the prayers and support of family and friends to slowly help me improve.

My employment agreement with Medtronic ran through 1998. However, their personnel policy allowed employees to retire at the age of fifty-seven and a half if they'd served a sufficient number of years. I met with Glen Nelson and Art Collins, to whom I reported, and explained my situation. They reluctantly agreed I could retire in 1997, provided I had found my replacement, preferably someone with management experience within Medtronic. Ron retired the following year.

Widdicomb remained in trouble. Remember the four reasons I'd purchased the company? The last two reasons—I thought I could afford it and it would be fun—were already dying in 1997 and were entirely proven wrong by 1999. Any possibility of fun had been decimated by my struggle with depression.

Yet as we entered 2001, we'd successfully changed the culture to a healthy one and established a high level of trust between ourselves and the employees. The employees voted to decertify their long-time union even though we'd reduced the number of employees by 50 percent.

We needed to have shipments of $43,000 a day to break even, and we were close to that level when the tragedy of 9/11 struck the World Trade Center twin towers in New York City. Orders immediately dropped to less than $6,000 a day and stayed there for months. Our furniture was sold primarily through designer showrooms located close to Ground Zero, and the accompanying blast had decimated them. I'd also bought out my partners and hired a new manager to run it.

The dollar loss up to that point was many times the purchase price of the company and had far exceeded my capability or interest in continuing to invest more money.

After I purchased the John Widdicomb Company, I soon learned my "golden finger" award, which my managers at DLP, Inc., had given me because everything we'd touched seemed to have turned to gold—had tarnished; instead, everything I touched seemed to be full of dry rot.

John Widdicomb's financial picture had changed over the intervening three-year period, and the bank had called the operating loan. I had borrowed heavily, and although a portfolio of my investments secured the loan, in 2001 the bank notified me they would not be renewing the loan. Banks across the nation were reducing their risk exposure. In 2000 and 2001, they were operating in a crisis mode all across the country. Low risk is the key to good banking relationships in running any business, and John Widdicomb was still a high-risk company.

In late 2001, my Widdicomb manager, Bob Dillon, and I evaluated the situation and determined we had to either sell or close the company.

GOD SENDS RESCUE

In spring 2002, Bob and I were exhibiting at the furniture market in High Point, North Carolina. We hoped to find a way to pay off the two-million-dollar loan before it came due by finding a company interested in purchasing the John Widdicomb Company while we were there.

One morning before the opening of the weeklong show, I was in my hotel room having a rug prayer time. I call it a rug prayer because God had brought me to a point where I was flat on the floor with my face buried in the rug, crying out to Him for help. My business life was a disaster.

The Bible says this about disaster: "Disaster will be inescapable, as if a man ran from a lion only to meet a bear, then escaped into a house, leaned his hand against the wall, and was bitten by a poisonous snake."[1]

I wasn't fighting a poisonous snake, but I felt I had a boa constrictor around my neck with no possible escape. After my prayer time, the Lord led me to this passage:

> I waited patiently for the LORD; he inclined to me and heard my cry. He drew me up from the pit of destruction, out of the miry bog, and set my feet upon a rock, making my steps secure. He put a new song in my mouth, a song of praise to our God. Many will see and fear, and put their trust in the LORD.[2]

This was a perfect description of how I felt, and it assured me that God was "standing by."

During the market, Bob found an Italian company that appeared to be seriously interested in purchasing John Widdicomb. The next day we met with the company and reached a letter of agreement for a sale. The agreement provided enough money to pay off the bank loans and promised good care for the employees—an answer to our prayers.

Shortly after the furniture market closed, the Italian company came to Grand Rapids with their attorney to work out the details of the contract. They promptly proceeded to ignore every employee protection we'd written into the letter of intent in High Point. By noon we were at a stalemate. I left for another meeting with an understanding between Bob, our attorney, and me—if the Italian company was unwilling to reinstate the employee protection clauses in the contract, the deal was dead.

The Italian company left for home that afternoon without the sale completed. It appeared as though the Lord had rescued us only to turn around and abandon us.

But He hadn't. Over the next several months, Bob worked with Jerry, my financial advisor, and they were able to liquidate the equipment. They also found the Stickley Company, which purchased the remaining assets and offered anyone who wanted them a job and a paid transfer to New York State to work in their manufacturing plant. The total funds we received were more than the Italian sale had offered. We were able to pay off the loan and provide more benefits to the employees than we'd initially thought, along with additional support in helping them find new jobs in the Grand Rapids area.

Five years later, after we'd both retired, Ron and I had an opportunity to spend some time with Bill George, the chairman of Medtronic. He told us DLP, Inc., was one of the companies they'd acquired that met the numbers and projections they used to evaluate the acquisition. From his perspective, the transition had been smooth, and DLP, Inc., continued to be a valuable addition to Medtronic.

In retrospect, some twenty-five years later, Ron and I still think it was the right decision for both the companies and our employees, many of whom still work for Medtronic or Medtronic suppliers. Medtronic has continued to service the cardiovascular surgeon's cannula needs, and the product line is now the largest of its kind in the world.

Now God had something new for me. But first I wrestled with the question of success.

CHAPTER TEN

REFLECTION AND NEW BEGINNINGS

D id my successful experiences make me a successful man? Scripture says Joseph was a successful man:

The LORD was with Joseph, and he became a successful man, and he was in the house of his Egyptian master. His master saw that the LORD was with him and that the LORD caused all that he did to succeed in his hands. So Joseph found favor in his sight and attended him, and he made him overseer of his house and put him in charge of all that he had. From the time that he made him overseer in his house and over all that he had, the LORD blessed the Egyptian's house for Joseph's sake; the blessing of the LORD was on all that he had, in house and field. So he left all that he had in Joseph's charge, and because of him he had no concern about anything but the food he ate.[1]

My experience and Joseph's were similar in many ways. The Lord had granted me and my associates success beyond all our expectations. Yes, we made mistakes, but our strong overall performance outweighed them. As I mentioned before, after we sold DLP, Inc., my managers gave me a "golden finger" award because everything we touched seemed to turn to gold. Like Joseph, I was a successful man.

But was I no longer a successful man, particularly in the Lord's eyes? God used my subsequent experiences to help me learn to look at my life through His eyes, not through my own.

For the next eighteen months, I struggled with the Lord over this question. Why had He blessed one business but the next one had been a total disaster? Finally, as I was praying one day, God brought to my mind a question from Him: *When you were in the medical business, did you draw closer to Me?*

I had to answer no. I became more independent.

Then He asked, *When you were in the furniture business, did you draw closer to Me?*

Oh, yes, I replied. *I was always on my knees, particularly when You seemed far removed and not willing to answer.*

Then God said, *In My eyes, what you called success was a failure and what you called failure was a success.*

Micah 6:8 says, "He has told you, O man, what is good; and what does the LORD require of you but to do justice, and to love kindness, and to walk humbly with your God?"

In Genesis chapters 37–50, Joseph was successful because the Lord was with him and made him succeed.[2] Success *happened* to Joseph. The closing verse of Genesis gives us Joseph's instructions to his brothers: "I am about to die, but God will visit you and bring you up out of this land to the land that he swore to Abraham, to Isaac, and to Jacob."[3]

Joseph lived to be 110, and he was forty years old when his father and brothers relocated to Egypt. However, Scripture tells us little about the latter half of his life. In Hebrews 11, though, he's mentioned in the roll call of faith: "By faith Joseph, at the end of his life, made mention of the exodus of the Israelites and gave directions concerning his bones."[4]

The Israelites were encouraged by Joseph's faith that looked forward and upward. And his story teaches us this: success is what happens *to* you; significance is what happens *through* you. This was what the Lord wanted to teach me. In His eyes I was not a failure; rather I was a success.

Here I was, sixty years old. I had achieved the American dream—starting a business with next to nothing, watching the Lord make it successful, winning significant awards from those observing me, changing my objective from how to keep a company growing to *How do I get out of this before it explodes?* I had earthly riches, but Ron Williams has a saying: "Rich makes you dumb." And I felt dumb.

Was it time to put up my feet and coast? No, I knew God had more opportunities waiting for me.

LIFE PLAN

Jim Buick, former president of Zondervan Publishing House, approached me one Sunday morning. He'd been trained by Tom Paterson, author of *Living the Life You Were Meant to Live*,[5] in how to do a Life Plan and wondered if I would be interested in going through the process. Strangely enough, I'd acquired a few questions over the last forty years and thought the process would give me some clarity! So I agreed.

I spent four workdays with Jim charting my life up to that point. I still had unresolved issues about leaving the ministry with Nicky Cruz Outreach and returning to the "secular" world and why there'd been such a contrast between the successes I saw at DLP, Inc., and my failure at John Widdicomb Company. But as Jim and I talked, a pattern emerged, which proved to me that God had been working all along behind the scenes to make all things right.

My final Life Plan exam was to create a presentation about the new insights I'd discovered and present it to Judy on Friday. The exercise also highlighted some of my passions: family, sculpture, India, pastors, leadership training, and my local church.

I found my relaxed schedule gave me time to be a caregiver for my daughter and my wife, who both struggled with cancer over the next six years. (Many fervent prayers were made and answered for both of them, and today they remain cancer free.) I also had time to pursue new interests. Let me tell you about some of them and how the Lord both led me and taught me.

SCULPTURE

My daughter, Lynda, and I were seated together for lunch at a ranch in Montana when she leaned over and said, "Dad, you haven't changed hobbies for six months. The sculptor who made these small bronze animals on the table will be here for supper. Why don't you sit next to him and see if you can learn something new?"

I did, and he invited me to join him at the corral the next morning to watch. But he did more than that. He supplied me with tools and clay so I could sculpt a horse. That kept me busy the rest of the week, and onlookers admitted that by the end of that week, my "creation" did look like an old swaybacked, worn-out horse. However, creating sculpture fascinated me. I had a new hobby.

Shortly after that, Dr. Rex Rogers, president of Cornerstone University at the time, asked if I would be interested in creating a sculpture to represent the days of creation and another to describe the fall. He wanted visual reminders on campus of the four-chapter gospel, and these would be the first two pieces. I designed and made two sculptures, one a set of bronze panels depicting the creation and the second a twice-life-size figurative sculpture depicting the fall.[6] We installed them on campus that October. They've also been installed on other university campuses, at camps, and in hospitals, as well as in Hyderabad, India.

The Lord has given me opportunities to share my sculptures in several venues over the succeeding years, and I'm excited when I receive a note or email that says the sender has been encouraged by God as a result of studying these sculptures.

INDIA

I joined Nicky Cruz Outreach in 1972. That same year my brother John was called to minister to India, and he founded Mission India (MI). As a result, he was always bugging me to travel there with him. My reply usually went something like *My guilt level is already high enough*, or *I don't think I need to go*, or *How about I support your ministry from here?* I did help with financial support for some of his major programs, but I was reluctant to visit the work.

However, in 1995, after I sold DLP, Inc., his pressure moved up a notch. I finally said, "If you can get Dale to go, I'll go." I anticipated my son-in-law would be a difficult sale. But two years later, John smiled and said, "I'm expecting you to go with Judy and Dale on our next tour." I was trapped.

It was early 1997, and I was still working for Medtronic. A vice presidents' meeting prevented me from flying with the tour group, so instead I had reservations through Frankfort to Delhi, a planned overnight in Delhi, and then a trek to Madras (now Chennai) the next day. The travel agent was to meet me at the Delhi airport, take me to a hotel, and get me back to the airport to catch my flight to Madras the next morning.

After landing at the airport in Delhi, I missed the travel agent, but I remembered someone saying I could catch a train to the regional airport. So I took the shuttle bus to the train station. However, when I arrived, it was the middle of the night, and the station was locked and closed. I spent the night "sleeping" on the steps outdoors with the beggars and homeless.

I was frightened; however, the Lord answered my prayers for protection. (I think He assigned a particularly patient and robust angel for me because He knew I'd test him from time to time.)

India is a beautiful country full of contrasts—gorgeous buildings and cardboard slums, the well-dressed businessperson and the beggar with deliberately malformed legs sharing the same street corner. Envision a driver in only a loincloth and a turban driving his oxcart while talking on a cell phone. You'll find innumerable people, cars, motor scooters, bicycles, and hand-drawn rickshaws all competing for a sliver of the roadway. Smoky fires emit an unforgettable vile smell that clings to you everywhere you go.

Sitting safely here in my study, I miss it. My wife, children, and grandchildren were fearful that after every trip I made to India and back, I would announce that "we" would be moving there.

This particular trip, John wanted to explore with me his vision for the Mission India national staff to have funds to support church planters. The Hindus were eager to have their children attend English-speaking schools, and the schools being Christian was not a factor in their minds. John's vision was to raise money to add additional classroom space and therefore accommodate more students. The school would then use some of the extra tuition to hire a church planter to minister to the Hindu students and their families.

By the end of that trip, I had committed to giving the largest financial gift I'd ever given, this time to expand several schools in Madras and the surrounding area. I left India feeling like the Lord had given me a new purpose.

When I returned to the States, I took the check to Mission India's headquarters and, with great joy, presented it to John. A week later, John told me the board wanted to place the money with the Foundation for New Era Philanthropy.[7] That foundation had promised to match the gift with donations from other foundations that wished to remain anonymous and then return the doubled funds to Mission India in three months. Mission India had experimented with this process involving several smaller amounts, and the Foundation for New Era Philanthropy had followed through. So I gave my permission.

My learning days were not over by any means. A few days later, the Foundation for New Era Philanthropy had collapsed. It had been a Ponzi scheme, and my donation was gone. The dream of expanded schools and support for church planters was no longer possible. But the Indian partners continued in unabated prayer for church planters and the schools.

Six months later, I was back in John's office with a new check for the original amount. I handed it to him and explained that I couldn't sleep. The Lord kept waking me up in the middle of the night.

Don't forget about your promise to the India schools, the Lord would say to me.

But I gave the money I promised.

Yes, but then you tried to show how clever you are by attempting to double the gift. In doing so, you robbed Me of the chance to show My power.

That's when I realized I needed to give again.

Over time, the Lord worked behind the scenes, and Mission India got about 80 percent of the first check back in addition to the new contribution.

I made several trips to India over the next few years and faithfully supported MI. During one trip, I talked with John about my burden to teach the leadership principles the Lord had taught me and was still teaching me to the young multi-vocation pastors there. Those pastors typically started a business to support themselves and their families and then pastored a church plant on the weekends.

"John," I said, "what do you think of this idea? I've written and tested two books on leadership with a group of inner-city businesspeople back in Grand Rapids. What if we had the books printed in India and started a new network of small-group studies to reach this key group of people?"

John thought it was a good idea. We had the books printed, and I traveled to India to work with a small group of pastors and medical doctors to watch them as they studied and discussed the first lesson of the course on leadership. The class was enthusiastic and wanted to meet again to explore the second lesson. They were even more excited than any of the students in my U.S. study group. Mission India then had the studies translated into several dialects and printed.

We also hired a representative to develop a distribution method and a website, but eventually we discovered he worked only when either John or I were in India and not at all when neither of us was. This was another great disappointment. His lack of performance was understandable when two employees revealed he was a closet alcoholic, but the losses incurred trying to make the John Widdicomb Company successful took away most of my funding capacity, and I had no money available to restart the project.

On another, earlier trip to India, John and I met with Pastor John Paul on a Sunday afternoon. As John and I drove up to his church, we saw a long line of mothers each holding a child, waiting patiently in front of the building. I asked John Paul if he was distributing medicine or food to them.

"I wish that were the case," he answered. "But these mothers can't afford to raise their children, so they're bringing them here. We can care for them in our orphanage—except for those who are physically or mentally disabled. I'm asking the Lord to help us start a new orphanage for them. But to prove to the Indian government we can successfully operate an orphanage for the disabled, we need to fund the orphanage for three years. After that, the government will reimburse us for all our incurred costs."

I whispered to John, "Ask him to give you a proposal." A few months later, John Paul sent my brother John the proposal. We supplied the funds, and the orphanage began operation. Three years later, it met the requirements for future funding from the Indian government and was now on a sound financial basis.

THE GREATEST AWARD

A month or so ago, Judy asked me this question (just as we were falling asleep, thanks a bunch): "Jim, over the years, you've been given awards by a wide range of organizations, some local and some national in status. Which award means the most to you?"

I couldn't give her an answer, and her question bothered me. But as I pondered it over the next weeks, a response began to form in my mind. None of those "public" awards meant the most to me. What did was a sentence or two from individuals the Lord put in my path—words only the two of us knew about.

A Widdicomb employee shared this with me: "I need to thank you, Jim. I've been watching you guide this company through good times and recently some terrible times. Yet you consistently put your employees first even though I know it came at a cost." Or a note saying, *I'm a changed person as a result of my coming to work here.* Or the smile on one little blind orphan girl's face in India. We were able to keep her off the streets of Mumbai because God's blessing made it possible for us to help her.

These are the reasons I continue to strive to lead—to hopefully be someone others can safely follow and get an occasional glimpse of our Lord and Savior along the way.

In telling my story here, I've included some of my life's joys, sorrows, duties, challenges, successes, and failures. To minimize any one of them would be minimizing God's truth as revealed in Scripture. It's easy to give comfort and encouragement, less so to talk about God's leading through difficulties and trials.

I trust this story will help you on your journey, and my wishes for you are found in these three Scriptures:

The LORD bless you and keep you; the LORD make his face to shine upon you and be gracious to you; the LORD lift up his countenance upon you and give you peace.[8]

We know that for those who love God all things work together for good, for those who are called according to his purpose.[9]

He has told you, O man, what is good; and what does the LORD require of you but to do justice, and to love kindness, and to walk humbly with your God?[10]

PART III
CREATING A HEALTHY CULTURE

Every organization has its own unique culture—a culture that builds or destroys, attracts staff or repels them, excites or puts one to sleep. But there's no such thing as a culture-less organization. An organization's culture is the composite of individual shared beliefs, attitudes, and values about their workplace.

Simply stated, an organization's culture is the way the organization as a group of individuals does things.

Now, you might think creating a healthy culture has something to do with structure. But think again. Have you heard this statement, part of it, or something like it? *Culture eats your structure for breakfast and your strategy for lunch.* I would express it this way: changing culture by reorganizing your structure is about as effective as attempting to make a hole in a bucket of water by sticking your finger into the water and then expecting the hole to remain when you remove your finger.

The cultures of teams, departments, divisions, and organizations all begin with leaders who day after day model the values they want to create. And their associates both within and without their sphere of influence watch them to see if they're acting according to those values. Culture doesn't grow spontaneously, and it needs reinforcement.

When I started DLP, Inc., we had the advantage of building a culture one employee at a time. The John Widdicomb Company's culture had been slowly damaged over the previous thirty years of operations, and the process of rebuilding it was entirely different. But whatever cultural opportunity you're currently facing or will face in the future, here are two foundational truths Rick and I have observed, and you need to recognize:

1. Leaders who have been in their organizations for an extended period tend to think they have created an ideal culture. But to determine the actual culture of their organizations, they need an evaluation by an independent assessor from outside the organization. What employees of an organization know the culture is and how the leaders of the same organization believe it is are often polar opposites.

2. Some students of leadership dismiss Christ-centered leadership as strictly a character-based leadership style of nominal value in the "real" world of organizations.[1] Maybe at some point, you have too. But other scholars observe this style of leadership develops characteristics that are common across all organizations with a positive culture.

In the following chapters we'll cover several characteristics of a healthy culture that members of organizations look for and that Christ-centered leaders must consider in order to foster a healthy culture. The first three are prayer, integrity, and authenticity.

CHAPTER ELEVEN

PRAYER, INTEGRITY, AND AUTHENTICITY

et's start with prayer. Again, the Bible begins with God asking *Where are you?* and ends with the world asking *Where is God?* As you model Christ-centered leadership, you'll help your associates discover the answer to the second question, and that requires prayer—prayer without ceasing.[1]

CHRIST-CENTERED LEADERS PRAY

Unless each morning you ask God to prepare you with the necessary skills, knowledge, integrity, and authenticity you need for that day, it will be difficult for you to reflect Jesus. You may think you need to be perfect if your associates are to be willing to follow you, but we've already covered that false notion. Perfection is an impossibility; we all drag our sins along everywhere we go. Thank goodness for God's grace!

But as we've already said, your faith, despite your imperfections, and your willingness to continue serving despite the obstacles you encounter are what provide the unique opportunity to reflect God's grace to others.

As a leader, you must have a deep trust in prayer. The Lord wants us to pray so He can use us as a living word picture to our associates. Psalm 40:3 says, "Many will see and fear and put their trust in the LORD." One way you show your trust in prayer is by sharing, without fanfare, the answers to your prayer with your associates.

For example, I had the coronary cannula I wrote about in my story, the one with the lawsuit over its patent, mounted in a display box hung on my office wall. It generated questions from others as well as daily reminding me that prayer makes a difference.

Let me share a few suggestions about prayer with you.

Seek a prayer partner outside of your organization.

Some years ago, a friend in New York asked if I would help a friend of his who had moved to Grand Rapids for a new job. The man had found that the firm he'd joined had financial problems, and because of the confidential nature of that situation, he needed someone he could trust to pray with. But being new to town, he didn't know anyone he could trust.

I reluctantly consented, thinking I didn't have the time but would give it a few weeks, meeting for about an hour each week. Our weeks of prayer, however, extended much longer than I'd anticipated. The requests regarding the financial "problem" were answered wondrously over the next few months, and by then we were so committed to praying with each other that we continued. We prayed for our problems at work, and we added prayers for our families and various needs.

Pray in detail.

Remember the incident I shared about Nicky Cruz Outreach not having enough money to meet payroll when I joined the organization? My prayer was clear and detailed: *Lord, we need the money to make the payroll on Friday.* He answered by supplying the need—and generously!

Pray even when it seems like God isn't answering.

Back to that lawsuit over the patent on the coronary cannula . . . I'm a control freak by nature, and the case was dragging on, costing DLP money it didn't have available. Over the months, the more I prayed, the worse the situation seemed to get. Even the court system was against me, it seemed. It was a dark time, and God wasn't answering my prayers—at least not the way I wanted Him to.

But the Lord dwells in deep darkness; in fact, the darker it seems, the closer He is. We may not see Him, but He's there. First Kings 8:10–12 tells us "when the priests came out of the Holy Place, a cloud filled the house of the LORD, so that the priests could not stand to minister because of the cloud, for the glory of the LORD filled the house of the LORD." Solomon stated, "The LORD has said that he would dwell in thick darkness." Solomon couldn't see God because God chose to protect him from His majesty.

David said something similar: "He made darkness his covering, his canopy around him, thick clouds dark with water."[2] David was often in distress and called out to the Lord: "In my distress I called upon the LORD; to my God, I cried for help. From his temple he heard my voice, and my cry to him reached his ears."[3]

We can't trust in our feelings. We need to realize God is by our side in the darkness.

We see this illustrated in 1 Kings 19. As the prophet Elijah cowered in a cave, depressed about recent events and Ahab and Jezebel's intent to kill him, God asked him what he was doing there. Elijah confessed his concerns, then said, "I, even I only, am left, and they seek my life, to take it away,"[4] implying God had deserted him. God told Elijah to stand on the mountain, and then He sent a windstorm, followed by an earthquake, and then fire.

Scripture tells us God wasn't "in" those powerful events, but He was there, with Elijah. Elijah just didn't seem to realize that, and he missed God's answer.

Then Elijah heard God whisper, effectively saying, *I the Lord am in control.* God assured Elijah He was there, not by making Himself visible or by showing His power but through His quiet whisper.

We can all feel desperate at times. Sometimes God answers my concerns and fears in power, and I see His answer. Then other times, He responds in a low whisper, and I have to stop being scared long enough to hear Him—or stop trying to find my own solution long enough to listen to Him.

Are you ever so scared or busy seeking a solution to a problem on your own that you miss His soft whisper?

Pray like a child.
The wisdom of praying like a child lies in its simplicity. The paradox of praying like a child is that complete trust is a sign of spiritual maturity. Yet this is hard for me to do. God loves to hear from children because they come in humility and trust. Stop and think about this, Jesus came to earth as a child and addressed the LORD as His father. Why should we think we can approach Him with any other attitude?

God wants to hear from us in sincerity, not necessarily in a carefully prepared speech outlining all the options we think He has available. How many of our planned activities today focus on worries that are beyond our control? Still, are we driven to handle them ourselves, or are we interested in the personal recognition they may bring if we solve them on our own?

Did I just hear a voice saying this? *Jim, if you truly believe in the power of prayer, maybe you shouldn't postpone praying!*

CHRIST-CENTERED LEADERS MODEL INTEGRITY

Leaders quickly learn that personal integrity is necessary to develop trust with their associates. Integrity in leaders refers to being honest and reliable. Leaders with integrity act according to their words—

they practice what they preach. And they own up to their mistakes as opposed to hiding them, blaming someone else, or making excuses.

Integrity is demonstrating that your beliefs, your words, and your actions are in harmony. Managers and business owners, whether or not they're Christ-followers, universally conclude that integrity is necessary if one is to build a relationship of trust within an organization. If even those who don't follow Christ believe integrity is the key to trust, shouldn't we who strive to follow Him seek to build integrity into our lives?

Handling Success

How you handle rewards and accolades is a measure of your integrity. Rewards are not wages due; they're gifts. They're an extraordinary honor for performance rendered.

As a leader, do you carefully and accurately communicate everyone's contribution? If you deserve a portion of a reward or accolade, do you acknowledge that you made a contribution and not brush it off with false modesty? Do you express gladness and joy when a follower receives a reward, or are you focused only on yourself?

Committing to Justice

Your commitment to justice is one of the ways to demonstrate your integrity. Do you look for injustice within your organization and try to rectify it? You verify your integrity by the way you handle small discrepancies. Often, leaders are required to make uncomfortable decisions or to correct wrongdoings. It may be a problem between two employees, or perhaps a customer or client with a real or imagined concern that needs sorting out.

If you're to be a witness for Christ, you must be careful not to play favorites or ignore issues of fairness. Yet this can happen all the time, particularly in a dynamic organization. For example, are you letting one customer continue to take a discount for prompt payment even when he pays late while not giving the same courtesy to long-time customers who routinely pay on time?

Refusing to make the uncomfortable call is a lack of integrity. We expect leaders to make decisions. Some are easy, but decisions involving personnel can be the most difficult. It's difficult to tell someone their work is unsatisfactory, so we procrastinate and then hope they leave the organization so we can avoid confronting them. But letting poor performance continue leads to a state of "satisfactory underperformance" and affects the rest of the personnel.

A cautionary note: Society at large is moving to redefine justice. Since everyone uses the same terms to describe what they mean when they say "justice," we may become complacent. Everyone is committed to equality, diversity, and inclusion, but the meaning of those words can be drastically different from one person to the next.

For most Christians, equality, diversity, and inclusion describe *biblical* justice. But others may be describing justice as *social* justice in terms of oppressors, repression, and redistribution of power to change outcomes to a more "just" basis.

Committing to Openness

Talking with employees about the possibility of having to close the John Widdicomb Company was difficult, but being upfront about it allowed each person to begin making adjustments or accept a job offer they might not have considered otherwise. Being open about the bad news helped to maintain a supportive culture through these difficult times.

CHRIST-CENTERED LEADERS MODEL AUTHENTICITY

Any attempt to model a healthy culture won't be recognized if you're fake. We reveal our authentic selves not by trying to appear perfect and certainly not by copying other leaders because we think that's what others expect of us. When we copy others, we hide our true selves. The media has manufactured a world out of people pretending to be saints and artificial heroes and then made them bigger-than-life Christians. Like the Kardashians, the only thing some well-known Christians are known for is that they're well known.

Becoming an authentic leader is not learning a style of leadership. Authentic leaders have serving others as their goal. They don't seek power; instead, they share their "power" by empowering others. Authentic leaders understand their abilities and shortcomings while leading with integrity because they value long-term relationships. They have a genuine connection to themselves, to their peers, and to their God.

Jesus was the exact imprint of God's nature.[5] If we are to be authentic followers of Christ, we need to reflect an accurate picture of Him to the best of our ability. And we must do so in a way that points others to Him, not to ourselves. Even with the Holy Spirit's help, we at best are a poor reflection of Jesus.[6]

Others will see the authentic "you," again with all your bumps, bruises, and shortcomings. But that won't stop them from accepting you as their leader. And as said earlier in the book, because of your authenticity, you'll no doubt touch some lives that may never catch a glimpse of Christ otherwise!

CHAPTER TWELVE

CONSISTENCY, TRUSTWORTHINESS, AND REFLECTING JESUS

In this chapter we'll cover another three factors in creating a healthy culture—consistency, trustworthiness, and perhaps the most important of all, reflecting Jesus.

CHRIST-CENTERED LEADERS ARE CONSISTENT

After reading my life story, you know my purchase of the John Widdicomb Company was a train wreck, a total disaster from a business standpoint! We had to shut down the company after it had been in business for more than a hundred years, and I lost a significant sum of money.

I was standing on the loading dock along with Mark, one of my managers, watching the last truck leave. He turned to me and said, "Jim, I need to thank you." I wondered what in the world was going on. This young manager had just lost his job through no fault of his own. He had a family to support, and it looked like he would need to move them to another town. I thought, *He feels he needs to thank me for what? I need to thank him, not the other way around!*

Mark continued. "I need to thank you because I've been watching you. When the company was going well, you treated us fairly and put your employees first. When things were bad, you treated us the same way. You've made sure we were treated generously at your expense. You went out of your way to help us in any way you could, even though you were personally facing tough times. When I came to work for you, I wondered, *How will Jim treat us if things turn bad?* Now I know the answer. Thank you for being consistent during both good and bad times!"

To be seen consistent in our actions is a high mark. Like others, I'm susceptible to being inconsistent. However, I've found that when I mess up, a sincere apology and requesting forgiveness helps to restore trust.

CHRIST-CENTERED LEADERS ARE TRUSTWORTHY

Jesus was believed in the world, and He asked His Father to send many more believers so others would realize God had sent Him.[1] To be believable, we need to be trustworthy; we need to keep our promises. Be a someone who carries through on what you say and promise. Small inconsistencies or failures to keep your word may result in damaging the trust others have in you. You will be judged untrustworthy.

Have you ever had a relationship someone destroyed this way? The destruction probably started with a small, almost insignificant misrepresentation by the other person. You then noticed a pattern beginning. You asked about the inconsistencies, but there was no explanation and no apology.

Trust decreases until it's gone.

An article in *Inc. Magazine* caught my eye. It was about a pricing inconsistency noticed by the person doing the invoicing for a small firm. A newer customer who qualified for a discount was told about it and got it. But an older customer who also qualified for the discount—and had for some time—was never even informed about it. The author of the article asked why this happened. Was it an oversight or a deliberate failure?

As followers of Christ, what would Jesus expect of us? As leaders, we seldom realize that people are watching us to determine if we're trustworthy in our dealings with others. Could a small inconsistency like the one mentioned above damage your reputation as a leader? Yes, it could.

CHRIST-CENTERED LEADERS REFLECT JESUS

We've already said reflecting Jesus is foundational to everything a Christ-centered leader does, but let's talk about how it specifically relates to creating a healthy culture.

About two years after we closed the John Widdicomb Company, I took some of my grandchildren to see a movie. As I was standing in the theater's lobby, I saw Fred pushing his way through the crowd to get to me. "Jim," he said, "I worked for you at the furniture company, and I just wanted to let you know I accepted the Lord a few months ago. The way you ran the company and the way you closed it down had a lot to do with starting my search for a God like yours. Thank you."

As I listened to him, it crossed my mind that his comments represented significance rather than success. The success of the furniture company would have been something happening to me, but perhaps the change in Fred's life came about in part because of the hope of Christ he saw reflected in me.

Our contemporaries are interested in spiritual matters, often looking for hope. And Jesus left us with the Great Commission, which requires us to teach others in a way that both helps them prepare for Christ's return and creates a culture of looking forward to the future with eagerness and optimism. But above all, reflect Jesus.

CHAPTER THIRTEEN

APPRECIATION, EQUAL TREATMENT, AND COMMON GRACE

How we treat others and communicate how God treats them are key to our success in creating a healthy culture. This is an important chapter, so please don't skip it thinking you already know all about appreciation, equal treatment, and showing God's common grace. You might just find some new and practical steps to take.

CHRIST-CENTERED LEADERS APPRECIATE OTHERS

In a blog post titled "The 5 Real Reasons Why Good Employees Quit," the number one reason given is not feeling appreciated.

> There are few things more demotivating for an employee than to feel unappreciated—as if their work doesn't matter...[and] this can be the fastest way to losing a valued employee . . .

Studies have shown that employees that feel they are valued and that are inspired [by] their job, are more likely to stay . . . Job satisfaction is a more important factor towards lesser employee churn than salary.[1]

In another recent report, 66 percent of employees surveyed said they would leave their jobs if they felt underappreciated. The number jumped to 76 percent for millennials.[2] Routinely expressing gratitude is revolutionary in an organization, and appreciation is the best weapon leaders have against losing good employees.

I was touring DLP, Inc.'s offices in Paris when I asked Jacques, our European manager, a question. "Every time I'm here, I notice you stop by each employee's desk and talk with them for a minute before you go to work. Why do you do that?"

He replied, "I'm telling them I appreciate their being here today. Americans are always in too much of a hurry. An executive from a large U.S. corporation was sent to Paris two years ago. I found him to be personable and a good leader. However, the employees asked that he be sent back to the States after his first year. The reason they gave was 'He never shows us appreciation.'" So make appreciation a priority. Showing others appreciation also keeps pride, the destructor of relationships, from taking hold of you.

The more leaders model appreciation, the more like Christ they become. Live out these two Scripture verses as your followers observe you:

"Give thanks in all circumstances; for this is the will of God in Christ Jesus for you."[3]

Give thanks to the LORD; call upon his name; make known his deeds among the peoples![4]

Scripture also tells us, "Bad company ruins good morals,"[5] so seek out grateful people as well. Their gratitude multiplies while ingratitude destroys.

CHRIST-CENTERED LEADERS TREAT OTHERS EQUALLY—AND WELL

Does your assistant have more flexibility in following procedures than a "regular" employee? If so, that's a clear indication you're not valuing everyone by the same measure. You need to convey that every employee is important to you through your actions. Share your concern for each one even while you carefully maintain the distinction that you are the leader.

How do employees feel valued? Here are a few ways.

When they receive fair wages and benefits

Paying a fair wage—paying the same level of salary—for comparable positions across an organization and providing benefits across the board are topics that fill books and seminars.

If we are to be witnesses for Christ, we must be careful not to ignore issues of fairness. Are you paying two people different wages for positions that have equal responsibilities? Are you treating all levels of your employees with benefits like health insurance, profit sharing, flex time, vacation, and sick time? Or do you hire employees for thirty hours per week to avoid paying benefits? Possibly discriminating against that single mother who needs benefits but can't find forty-hour-a-week employment?

If you first concentrate on being fair to your lowest-level employees, proper treatment of the other levels will quickly follow.

When their leaders listen to them

We'll talk more about meaningful communication later, but we all feel valued when someone focuses on what we're saying. Nothing is more demeaning than knowing the other person is already preparing an answer before you've even completed your explanation. And actions like having one eye on your cell phone before giving the other person a full hearing while at the same time demanding they hear you is disastrous and belittling.

You may have heard this often-told story about three construction workers. One day, a passerby asks them what they're doing. The first one says, "I'm doing what the foreman tells me to." The second one says, "I'm breaking big rocks into little ones." Then the third one, whose task is sweeping up after the others—and who recently received an Employee of the Month award, thanking him for his contribution—answers with pride, "I'm building a cathedral!"

Which worker do you think has higher job satisfaction? Works harder? Contributes more to the success of the project? The difference between the three construction workers isn't the task they're performing; it's the story they're living. Being recognized for their contribution encourages employees to value their work, in a way similar to *I'm building a cathedral!*

When they know their leader is committed no matter what

Commitment and having the will to succeed are two sides of the same coin. Commitment shows up when tested. Sometimes leading is discouraging and difficult.

When we see one of our followers make substantial growth, it brings us great joy. But to experience that kind of pleasure, we need to commit to leading through difficult times. The Bible talks about shepherd leaders, a style of leadership we mentioned earlier in the book. A committed shepherd tends, gathers, carries, leads, protects, and guides through all circumstances. Being a true shepherd requires commitment.

But commitment costs us something. It requires sacrifice. We must be motivated by an obligation to give up something of ours that isn't replaceable voluntarily. Our sacrifice may involve one or more of the following: time, emotional energy, vulnerability, or risking our reputation by taking an unpopular stand. Jesus, our Shepard Leader, laid down His life for us. In our work, are we committed to anything close to this level of sacrifice?

Commitment to our followers means we must be ready to teach, ready to empower, ready to comfort, ready to govern, and ready to stabilize. When nothing is going smoothly or we're in the middle of a crisis, we can't walk away or close our office door and hide. In assuming the role of leader, we've committed to keeping our followers safe and protected.

CHRIST-CENTERED LEADERS SHOW GOD'S COMMON GRACE

What is inclusivity? It's accepting others in the workplace without condemnation and discrimination. It's showing that you welcome everyone as equally valuable to the organization. It's showing you value diversity for the strength it gives an organization. It's allowing for God's common grace.

In no area is this more important than working with nonbelievers. By showing grace to them, you create a way for them to hear the message of Christ. Common grace is the gift of God by which He gives all people, even His enemies, undeserved blessings. God wants you to work alongside others who may not be followers of Christ, so you will have an opportunity to show His common grace to them.

It's a leader's responsibility to establish sound policies and standards for use in the workplace. Your organization will undoubtedly have rules and guidelines that need to be followed. You will need to apply them fairly and without personal bias. But if you allow any of your personal beliefs to enter into this decision, you open yourself to the possibility of accusations of unfairness. Ensure you have accurate, complete, and documented information before you take any action.

God never calls a believer to judge a nonbeliever. According to Jesus, it is the Holy Spirit's responsibility to convict the person, not our own: "When [the Holy Spirit] comes, he will convict the world concerning sin and righteousness and judgment."[6]

Jesus also said,

> Judge not, that you be not judged. For with the judgment you pronounce you will be judged, and with the measure you use it will be measured to you. Why do you see the speck that is in your brother's eye, but do not notice the log that is in your own eye? Or how can you say to your brother, "Let me take the speck out of your eye," when there is the log in your own eye? You hypocrite, first take the log out of your own eye, and then you will see clearly to take the speck out of your brother's eye.[7]

This Scripture passage refers to another member of God's family, male or female, who is to be rebuked, in private or outside your workplace by someone else, with love after verification of an offense. But we often stop with verse 5 and miss the continuation of this paragraph, verse 6: "Do not give dogs what is holy, and do not throw your pearls before pigs, lest they trample them underfoot and turn to attack you."[8]

Verse 6 is a warning that tells us if we judge someone who is currently not a follower of Christ, we are wasting our time, and we can expect the other person to turn and attack us if we attempt to judge them.

Treating everyone as an equal recipient of common grace will build relationships and keep the door open for them to ask you about spiritual matters, in God's time.

CHAPTER FOURTEEN

DEVELOPING MEANINGFUL COMMUNICATION

W e all think we know a lot about communication, and maybe we do. But have we learned how to make it truly meaningful for leaders and followers alike? How do we do that?

MEANINGFUL COMMUNICATION REQUIRES MEANINGFUL RELATIONSHIPS

Ideally, the workplace functions as a community. Earlier, we defined an organization's culture as the composite of individuals sharing beliefs, attitudes, and values about their workplace.

Relationships within a community develop with time provided to interact, a level of trust between individuals, and accurate communication, hopefully beyond video conferences. Leaders need to show they value these kinds of relationships by deliberately creating opportunities for them to develop and encouraging them to grow.

OPENNESS MATTERS

Your followers deserve accurate and timely communication—of both good news and bad news. If you don't provide that, you'll break down the trust necessary for good communication. Some things you cannot disclose to everyone; however, when they suspect or know something is going on, acknowledge the problem and say you will fully inform them as soon as possible. Then follow through on that promise.

HONESTY AND ACCURACY MATTER

When giving a performance review to an employee, don't gloss over their performance. If they did poorly, they already know it. Discuss how they can improve.

For years, I never felt I'd received a useful performance review by the person to whom I reported. I was given a *Thanks for a good [or even great] job* and *Jim, your next year's salary is . . . See you next year.*

Then I was given an annual review by Art Collins, who was at that time CEO of Medtronic. Art laid it out for me plainly, all my bumps and warts along with my strengths. It was terrific how energizing that review was for me and how encouraging it was for me because he took an extensive amount of his time to be thorough.

METHODOLOGY MATTERS

At one point, I thought I was communicating DLP, Inc.'s values and goals by giving an impassioned speech at our semi-annual employee meeting. Then my eyes were opened.

When on a trip to India, I picked up a book on communication. Unfortunately, I didn't buy the book and I can't remember the title or author, but I noticed a paragraph that said something like this: *Distrust and miscommunication are often rampant between different levels of employees, and it's impossible to communicate to a diverse group of employees just by speaking to them.*

The author then followed with this observation: *When facilitated by the leader of a small group, communication within an organization is the most accurate. People who work closely together build a culture of trust with one another.*

The main thing I retained from the book is that if we're to communicate well within an organization, we must develop a high level of trust in the messenger and have a method of accurately communicating with every employee throughout the organization.

Here are a few other nuggets of wisdom I remember from that book:

- Communication within a perceived chain of command carries additional unspoken connotations along with the message.
- Critical words from a superior create wounds far beyond what they intended to communicate.
- Position within an organization creates both barriers and biases. Hourly workers, for instance, frequently discount "management" statements as always being untrue or at least offered from a selfish or company perspective.
- The greater the perceived "distance" in responsibility between the sender and the receiver, the more likely the message will be filtered out and fall on deaf ears.
- "All-company" meetings are examined for hidden meanings and are seldom remembered once over.
- The same type of barriers exists in the reverse direction. Employees may not express themselves to their manager because they fear rejection, they have a poor self-image, they've had an emotional reaction to the way the manager reacted in the past, or any number of other reasons.

Improving at DLP, Inc.

It was clear to me that if we were to build and maintain a desirable culture within DLP, Inc., we needed a new way to communicate to everyone across the organization and enhance the level of trust that continued from the time we were a startup organization. That book's message—that the receiver is most likely to hear a message from someone they trust and who communicates with them regularly—was clearly expressed.

When I returned from that trip, I shared these concerns with Ron. Then we changed our whole method of communicating within DLP, Inc.

Ron and I had developed a high level of trust between ourselves and the leaders of naturally formed teams because we worked closely with them. In turn, their associates trusted them. We began communicating through these leaders, and they, in turn, conveyed the message to their groups. No more PowerPoint presentations. No more mass meetings to attempt to communicate values and goals—and the smaller the group, the better.

Improving at John Widdicomb Company

As I've said, when I purchased the John Widdicomb Company, it had a terrible culture. Trust was nonexistent at all levels of the organization, particularly between managers and those they supervised. Nor was there any efficient and accurate way to communicate across the organization.

So we put together our action plan, addressing the company culture in two areas, both top priorities: improving trust levels and improving the accuracy of communication. You know from my story that we were eventually successful.

COMMUNICATION SKILLS MUST BE DEVELOPED

God gave us the gift of communication, and there is absolutely no way to build relationships without it. Relationships enhance communication because it has to be a two-way street to be meaningful. It requires both parties to speak and listen. If we only talk and don't listen, we don't communicate. And that's why communication skills must be developed.

When we pray, God urges us to "be still, and know that I am God,"[1] so we can hear from Him. An organization's culture must provide a safe place for two-way communication with both positives and negatives without the threat of punishment or unhelpful, undue praise. And no actual communication can take place without a high level of trust. That's why confidence in our followers and their trust in us is essential.

Communicate with Accuracy

Accurate communication is a learned skill, and my inability to always communicate accurately was driven home to me one spring. I'm a gardener, and when I needed some additional help, my daughter recommended her friend Tim. But it soon became apparent that he was not an experienced gardener.

Some small bushes had dark-green leaves left from the previous year's growth as well as new pale-green leaves from the spring growth, and I wanted the young development cut off. I gave Tim instructions, and then I left. When I returned home that night, there were these new "twiggy" things I hadn't seen before. Tim had picked all the green leaves off each bush, one by one.

Well, I hadn't differentiated between the two kinds of leaves. I'd just said, "remove the green from these bushes," and green is green.

Can you imagine Tim's angst? It was a dumb instruction on my part, but why pick all the leaves from a healthy bush? He wanted to do a thorough job, which he did. I'd just omitted one word in my instructions—*pale*.

Communicate with Stories

I recently finished a class on telling stories,[2] where I learned that our brains are programmed to receive information in the form of stories even before birth. Our brains use stories to understand and create meaning from the world around us. We think in story form, we create meaning in story form, we sense in story form. We remember and recall information through the use of stories.

However, if the story isn't complete or is entirely different from our expectations, our minds will modify the story without our realizing it. It may change (even reverse) factual information; make assumptions; create new knowledge; ignore parts of the provided information; infer connections and information; assume motive, intent, and significance; and invent further information and detail.[3]

For example, if I say, "Luke was alone when he rang the neighbor's doorbell," your brain will infer, assume, elaborate, interpret, and project information that makes sense to you based on your prior experiences. What did you assume after reading that sentence?

I would assume Luke was lonely and wanted company. But you might have assumed he was up to no good. No wonder achieving clear and accurate communication is difficult.

So, to ensure what you say is accurately heard, make sure your "story" is complete and clear, and then ask the listener what they heard to be sure you're on the same page.

THE SPIRITUAL DIMENSION AND PERSONAL BIAS CAN BE BARRIERS

Based on the story of Babel, we know there were once no barriers to communication such as we have today:

The LORD came down to see the city and the tower, which the children of man had built. And the LORD said, "Behold, they are one people, and they have all one language, and this is only the beginning of what they will do. And nothing that they propose to do will now be impossible for them. Come, let us go down and there confuse their language, so that they may not understand one another's speech."[4]

Zephaniah prophesies that someday the Lord will remove the communication barrier He put into place and all God's people will once again speak with a single, purified language to work in one accord to bring about the conversion of all nations.[5]

Sin has placed barriers in communication and created alienation between individuals and between individuals and God. Communication has also become a way to inflict pain. Proverbs 12:18, however, gives us hope: "There is one whose rash words are like sword thrusts, but the tongue of the wise brings healing." We need to be particularly careful as leaders, because our reckless words—if derived from our religious beliefs, a position of authority, or spoken to someone who trusts us—can devastate associates.

Then we have the matter of personal bias. We've all developed biases, making it a challenge to accept ideas that contradict our prejudices. These biases may be a result of personal interests and needs; differences in language, culture, religion, or worldview; distrustful relationships with specific individuals or groups; and "road closed" signs in areas where we've experienced hurt. Information directed toward us is never genuinely heard and received if it doesn't make it through these barriers.

Understand that your followers may have a different perspective from yours, and until both views align, you may not be able to understand one another correctly.

Jesus's disciples didn't understand everything He taught, but after His resurrection, they understood more of what He was saying to them.

> The Jews said to him, "What sign do you show us for doing these things?" Jesus answered them, "Destroy this temple, and in three days I will raise it up." The Jews then said, "It has taken forty-six years to build this temple, and will you raise it up in three days?" But he was speaking about the temple of his body. When therefore he was raised from the dead, his disciples remembered that he had said this, and they believed the Scripture and the word that Jesus had spoken.[6]

A FINAL NOTE

Meaningful communication is so vital that we've included two pieces at the end of this book to help you increase your skills. The first, about communicating responsibly, is from Rick, and the second, about learning from Jesus, the master communicator, is from Michelle Sessoms.

CHAPTER FIFTEEN

EFFECTIVELY MANAGING CHANGE

We can't get away from change, but we can help our coworkers cope with the changes they face.

Many organizational changes are forced on us by major catastrophes like 9/11 or COVID-19. Some changes are positive for members of an organization, like being promoted. But some changes are viewed negatively. For instance, more sales may be considered negative by those responsible for completing supporting tasks, while the leaders think it's great because of increased stability and earnings. Either way, both positive and negative change must be managed.

PLAN FOR TIME AND COMMUNICATION

Plans for a pending change should allow for sufficient time to communicate the change and its impact. The longer the time allowed for communication and participative discussion before the change, the better. Leaders need to understand that adjusting to change is a process that requires time.

Earlier in Rick's career, he eagerly embraced his leadership responsibility to initiate change. In fact, he liked change—change he initiated, that is. But over time he came to realize he wasn't so receptive to change someone else was initiating.

This awareness led him to appreciate the challenging process of leading people through change. In more recent years as CEO of Freedom to Lead International, he has not only altered his approach to leading change but teaches leaders around the world about leading change.

Most people are uncomfortable with change something or someone else initiates. Even good change often brings a sense of loss and grief. In fact, the experience of change is akin to the loss and grief associated with death and dying. When change occurs, something dies in order for something else to be born.

The late Dr. *Elisabeth Kübler-Ross* identified the five stages of grief associated with death and dying:

1. Denial
2. Anger
3. Bargaining
4. Depression
5. Acceptance

The problem is that leaders often tend to skip over the stages of grief and expect people to accept the new people or project or strategy or office layout immediately. This can result in people getting stuck in their perceived loss and being unable to engage positively in the change.

Rick has found several ways to help people through the change process:

Embrace grief. Remember that grief during change is natural. By understanding the process of loss and grief, we can lead the change instead of allowing resistance to the change to lead us.

Accept emotions. Grief isn't talked about much in the workplace because it's an emotional reaction to loss, not an intellectual one. Leaders can encourage the change process and reduce resistance by creating safe environments for people to express their emotions.

Slow down. Resist the mantra that "speed is king." It takes time for people to process the feelings associated with loss that come with change.

Move forward together. It's important that people don't wallow indefinitely in grief and become chronic complainers. Engage other influencers to communicate the positive aspects of the change initiative.

With a commitment to cultivate others to reach their highest potential, these pointers to accommodate grief are essential during the change process

Whatever the situation you and your followers face, planning, time, and communication are all key. As Rick has just pointed out, we can anticipate that some of those affected by significant change will experience a sense of loss and some or all of the classical stages of grief. But leaders can address that sense of loss by communicating that the future rewards will be greater or at least acceptable compared to the loss. This sense of hope is often an incentive for an individual to not only accept the change but look forward to executing it.

ANTICIPATE CHALLENGE

Particularly if the change isn't voluntary, leaders should anticipate other challenges as well. In other words, expect some complaining.

God called Moses to lead the Israelites out of Egypt, but some rabble-rousers complained about not having the comforts of Egypt and wanted to turn back:

> The whole congregation of the people of Israel grumbled against Moses and Aaron in the wilderness, and the people of Israel said to them, "Would that we had died by the hand of the LORD in the land of Egypt, when we sat by the meat pots and ate bread to the full, for you have brought us out into this wilderness to kill this whole assembly with hunger."[1]

But some were not happy even after the Lord gave them manna to eat:

> Now the rabble that was among them had a strong craving. And the people of Israel also wept again and said, "Oh that we had meat to eat! We remember the fish we ate in Egypt that cost nothing, the cucumbers, the melons, the leeks, the onions, and the garlic. But now our strength is dried up, and there is nothing at all but this manna to look at."[2]

You need everyone's support for making a change or at least accepting the difference if it hasn't been voluntary. Leaders often minimize the importance of this stage. It may take months of reinforcement to get total acceptance. In Moses's case, it took years.

CELEBRATE

When a change is complete and accepted, a celebration is in order. Reinforcement follows approval. Don't stop at one announcement; communicate regularly as the transition progresses and new aspects emerge. For arduous changes establish milestones and celebrate each one.

In fact, has it been a long time since you've had a party? Make up some excuse and throw one! Doing so will help maintain and build the trust others have in you.

TEACH TEACHABILITY

Why is being teachable such an essential part of an organization's culture? Because a "living" organization must continually reinvent itself.

Resistance to change is fatal. The phrase *That's not the way we do it* closes doors to new opportunities, and better ideas will never surface. If we're not teachable, we become entrenched in our ways to the point where we believe we always know best, even to the extent of denying reality.

In business, as our customer or client base shifts, competitors introduce new products or services, and new ways to reach our markets develop. We should be continually searching for new ideas and new ways of doing business, and so must our followers

Another term for teachability is *adaptive capacity*. When combined with continued learning, adaptive capacity will increase creativity. Just as we said reflecting Christ can create a culture of looking forward with eagerness and optimism, which in turn increases hope, so, too, can both teachability and adaptive capacity. They enable people to recognize and seize new opportunities.

The goal of embracing and fostering a teachable spirit requires continual teaching. We refer to "teachable moments," but we forget that all our actions and words are teaching others something about our values and ourselves. If we expect our followers to be teachable, we must have a teachable spirit ourselves and encourage its development in others. Leaders fail when their followers become unteachable, and the organization's risk of eventually dying increases.

Now let's turn our attention to building and maintaining trust.

CHAPTER SIXTEEN

BUILDING AND MAINTAINING TRUST

I'm sure by this time you've noticed this book repeatedly emphasizes building trust—your followers' and associates' trust in your leadership and everyone's trust in each other. It's such an important charge that we recommend taking this step: before you take any action, ask yourself, *If I do this, will it increase or decrease the level of trust placed in me?*

Let's start with how sharing your own passion, motivation, and zeal builds trust, and then move on to the difference shared leadership and collaboration can make.

SHARE YOUR PASSION, MOTIVATION, AND ZEAL

Remember that accomplishing a task proceeds from a passion for the broader mission and is followed by motivation to accomplish the task, and then zeal turns motivation into action. And when your followers see all of this in you, you're building trust.

Passion

What is passion? How does it differ from being passionate? Henri Nouwen defines passion this way[1]: "Passion is a kind of waiting; waiting for what other people are going to do."

I had always thought of passion as an action, but it's a deep-in-your-bones commitment to accomplishing an objective. I had confused passion with being passionate. Passionate implies action and it's transitory. Passion is for the long haul. Passionate requires an immediate response; passion is willing to wait. Passionate results in emotions soon gone; passion moves mountains and produces changes. As leaders, we must show and share our love for the mission.

As followers of Christ, we are fortunate, because God gives us a passion for what He wants us to accomplish. Every time I've undertaken an activity or led the charge to implement a change without a passion for it, I've been disappointed with the outcome.

Matthew tells a story about a man who came to Jesus with this question: "Teacher, what good deed must I do to have eternal life?" After Jesus asked a series of questions concerning the commandments, the man replied, "All these I have kept. What do I still lack?" Then,

> Jesus said to him, "If you would be perfect, go, sell what you possess and give to the poor, and you will have treasure in heaven; and come, follow me." When the young man heard this, he went away sorrowful, for he had great possessions.[2]

The man wanted to be "good," but he had a love for riches. Although he departed disappointed, he at least seemed to understand that he lacked the passion for fulfilling the final challenge keeping him from reaching his goal.

Motivation

Motivation is energized, persistent, and goal-directed behavior. When we're motivated, we move and take action.

As Christ-centered leaders, what motivates us? What makes the follower of Christ who works in the workplace distinctive? You can examine a list of positive character traits and find most of them in other leaders. Still, the only authentic characteristic of someone who's a follower of Christ is the motivation to live in a way that others are drawn to Christ by their service to them. Our inspiration is to give, while the world is motivated by the opportunity to get.

In business, we demonstrate our motivation by providing the best possible value to our customers or clients while allowing our vendors and employees an opportunity to make a good living. Others may operate in the mode of maximizing revenue and minimizing expenses by taking advantage of others. But our motive is to invest in people, not ourselves. As Christ-centered leaders, we must share this motivation with others. They should clearly understand our reason is to serve our Leader and others, not just reaching a monetary goal.

We're motivated by the unique objective we've been given—reflecting Christ and serving others.

Zeal

I introduced zeal in an earlier discussion and cited my lack of zeal as being one of the major differences between successfully reaching a goal and failure. The New Testament refers to zeal as a sense of long-term commitment: "Do not be slothful in zeal, be fervent in spirit, serve the Lord."[3]

An example of zeal is Jesus's righteous anger when He cleansed the temple: "'[Jesus said] take these things away; do not make my Father's house a house of trade.' His disciples remembered that it was written, 'Zeal for your house will consume me.'"[4]

Zeal adds the idea that we should be so committed to our leadership role that we won't let anything stand in the way.

SHARED LEADERSHIP AND COLLABORATION

Every month, one of our continuous improvement teams at DLP, Inc., made a presentation to the "managers" and other team leaders. These teams were made up of volunteers from each department. They defined a problem, then made a list of what was making it difficult to reach their objectives. Then they jointly developed a solution and tested it. If it failed to provide a better answer to the problem, they made the necessary adjustments and tried again.

Listening to their monthly progress presentations became a humbling experience for me. I was overwhelmed with the depth of commitment and wisdom offered by those presenting. Morale, quality, and customer service improved while costs went down, and I learned I needed to wipe out my preconceived ideas about the effectiveness of teams.

The teams, working together, had more specific and more practical knowledge than I did. Fortunately, as time passed, the number of teams grew across every area of the company. They were the key to the success of the company, enabling it to reach its objectives.

Here are some ways you can make shared leadership and collaboration happen.

Delegate and Let Go of the Credit

When I was traveling for Baxter Laboratories, I was overwhelmed with managing development groups in three locations, and I complained to my friend Ed Bratcher, who was ministering in Chapel Hill, North Carolina. He was brutal with me. "You wouldn't be so bad off if you would delegate more. You're opinionated, and you believe no one can do it as well as you can." (That accusation is sometimes true, unfortunately). "Your problem might also be about who gets credit."

Then he told me this story:

> My days often become hectic, particularly with the demands created by calls from parishioners. One day a call came from a prominent church member who was in the hospital across town. His problem was serious but by no means an emergency. Still, he wanted me to drop everything and come visit him.
>
> This request placed me in a struggle with my inner desire to be recognized. It would take an hour to travel across town to the hospital and an hour back, all for a fifteen-minute visit in which I would pray for him for only a few minutes. Staying would certainly be more efficient, but would it be politically wise for me to go? Of course, I could spend the two hours traveling back and forth across town praying for the concerns of my whole congregation. But I was hesitant to do that because I wouldn't receive any acknowledgment for my efforts.

Ed's story comes to mind every time I look at a busy day ahead of me. How many plans are on my list because I want credit for them? And how does that affect my willingness to delegate to others? How many tasks don't I entrust to others because I lack trust in them? How many of today's activities focus on worries that are really beyond my control, yet I want to handle them myself rather than turn them over to God?

Am I like Ed, factoring personal recognition into my thinking?

I've worked hard to break this habit of wanting to take credit, particularly when it comes to delegating to others. Please, release opportunities for yourself to your associates. Trust them to deliver and forget about getting credit.

Don't Just Delegate—Empower

Part of a leader's responsibility is to provide followers with meaningful work. You can do that by empowering them and providing opportunities for new experiences.

The idea that empowering others robs us of power or influence is an untruth. Too often delegation means just asking someone to perform a specific task while we retain the power. We transfer the execution portion of the job but not the ultimate responsibility, which we want to keep. But true empowerment requires us to give the responsibility to the person who is completing the task. Empowering actually expands our impact as we delegate to subordinates.

True empowerment includes giving people the chance to exercise their decision-making ability, and it requires absolute trust in the individual by the delegator. Empowerment is illustrated by Jesus's reaction to the centurion's request to heal his servant:

> When [Jesus] had entered Capernaum, a centurion came forward to him, appealing to him, "Lord, my servant is lying paralyzed at home, suffering terribly." And he said to him, "I will come and heal him."
>
> But the centurion replied, "Lord, I am not worthy to have you come under my roof, but only say the word, and my servant will be healed. For I too am a man under authority, with soldiers under me. And I say to one, 'Go,' and he goes, and to another, 'Come,' and he comes, and to my servant, 'Do this,' and he does it."
>
> When Jesus heard this, he marveled and said to those who followed him, "Truly, I tell you, with no one in Israel have I found such faith. I tell you, many will come from east and west and recline at table with Abraham, Isaac, and Jacob in the kingdom of heaven, while the sons of the kingdom will be thrown into the outer darkness. In

that place there will be weeping and gnashing of teeth."
And to the centurion Jesus said, "Go; let it be done for
you as you have believed." And the servant was healed at
that very moment.[5]

The centurion requested Jesus's help and placed his trust
in Him. He offered Jesus a choice and accepted how He was to
accomplish what he needed. The centurion empowered Jesus to
heal his servant.

Existing training combined with empowerment prepares
an organization to function well during a time of crisis because
associates know they can make a decision within their area of
responsibility. Arriving at a consensus usually works okay. However,
it often requires time to achieve. If you typically lead using a
consensus management style, your followers need to understand a
crisis may require a different type of management. I understand U.S.
armed forces are moving toward more consensus management, but
they still retain a structure for making decisions in times of crisis.

Provide New Experiences
Marketing today emphasizes the experiential, and here's why:

> David Seel Jr., in his book *The New Copernicans*,[6] writes
> extensively about how millennials differ from earlier
> generations. He explains how today's marketing targets
> them, taking into account that they value experience. The
> priority of experience has educational and commercial
> implications because millennials prefer to process reality
> from hand to heart and then to head based on experience,
> imagination, and then analytic reason.
>
> We need to consider this orientation when selecting
> the way we lead. We need to reorient toward experimental
> learning and away from abstractions. Seel explains about

the "experience economy" and describes an increasing progression of economic value from commodities to making goods to delivering services to the "capstone"— staging experiences.

When we characterize our relationship with God as an experience, we're ignoring the message incorporated in the roll call of faith given in Hebrews 11, which ends with "and all these, though commended through their faith, did not receive"—or experience— "what was promised."[7]

Provide a Positive Atmosphere

People should be able to like where they work, and how decisions are made and disagreements are handled affect the atmosphere of a department or an organization. Unfair application of policy when a recipient is an obvious favorite or has unlimited access to supervisors are irritants. Unresolved personnel issues that drag on are open wounds.

At one time, I thought there was no permissible reason that allowed me to dismiss a divisive individual. Yet I struggled with how to deal with someone who repeatedly demonstrated divisiveness. Then I was shown this verse: "As for a person who stirs up division, after warning him once and then twice, have nothing more to do with him."[8]

Reward team builders. Treat those who are negative and divisive as having committed serious offenses.

Provide a Stable Structure

For an organization to function smoothly, it must have a stable structure, and just as President Harry Truman supposedly had a sign on his desk that said, *The buck stops here*, leaders are ultimately responsible for the stability of their organizations.

One of these responsibilities is managing followers, and to do that, we must be willing to accept the clear distinction between their roles and ours. As Christ-centered leaders, however, we can blur that distinction, making it easy to give our followers what they want instead of what they need.

Moses faced the need for responsible leadership when his time was coming to an end. He said to God,

> Let the LORD, the God of the spirits of all flesh, appoint a man over the congregation who shall go out before them and come in before them, who shall lead them out and bring them in, that the congregation of the LORD may not be as sheep that have no shepherd.[9]

Moses knew he needed God to appoint someone to help him manage the people, and God did. He appointed Joshua not only to help Moses but to succeed him. After all, any organization without a leader soon self-destructs.

Then when in Deuteronomy the people are being reminded of the laws they must obey, we read,

> You shall not do according to all that we are doing here today, everyone doing whatever is right in his own eyes, for you have not as yet come to the rest and to the inheritance that the LORD your God is giving you."[10]

Everyone needs direction and the stability to have the freedom to do their best. They need someone steadfast. If their leader continually changes direction—especially in a crisis—followers lose their reference point and are likely to charge off in the wrong direction. If leaders don't stabilize an organization, people fall back into old habits, to their comfort zone. They need to be guided by a leader they trust and respect.

Invest in Developing Others

If your followers are to be the leaders of tomorrow, they need a mentor or coach. They desperately want more-experienced leaders to walk alongside them, to help them discover underused strengths, maintain focus in the midst of hardship, eliminate blind spots, and master new challenges. Those you lead no longer view this kind of relationship as optional.

One of the primary responsibilities for any Christ-centered leader is developing their followers. The world is messy—disasters happen, diseases decimate, hopes are crushed, and trust is betrayed. When a leader encounters one of these obstacles, it's dangerous— particularly for the fledgling leader. They need a wise mentor to guide them.

One of the most painful experiences for me is to see someone I'm mentoring stumble. I constantly need to be watchful and ready to intervene. A vital responsibility of being a leader is to be a diligent mentor and coach.

When we deliberately invest ourselves in others, we create a culture of confidence and safety because our followers know they won't be standing alone when the unavoidable situation occurs. Associates not directly involved will see your steady commitment and be encouraged. Instead of discouragement spreading through your department or organization, hope takes its place.

I am indebted to mentors like Bernie from the grocery store, Dick Sarns, and my business partners Ron Williams and Hugh Cummings in particular. Rick has mentors as well. He names David Muir, his dear friend Colin Buckland, and above all, his dad as being key to his development as a leader.

Rick and I don't merit these relationships; they are a gift, freely offered. They formed us and changed us as leaders, and that obligates us, in gratitude, to in turn mentor and care for our associates.

Christ-centered leaders must be committed to relationships that hone effective leadership thinking, values, and behavior. Help, offered sincerely, is always welcomed because everyone wants a leader who cares, guides, and willingly chooses to give of themselves. In return they will be rewarded with an overwhelming sense of satisfaction.

Our purpose in mentoring is to lead our followers to use their talents and skills effectively. This requires us to develop a mutual sense of relationship, trust, safety, protection, and learning while recognizing there can be only one leader.

In turn, as leaders we can count on being tested for steadfastness and perseverance. Jesus was steadfast when tested for forty days in the wilderness. Noah persevered when day after day, for a hundred years, he built the ark in a place that had never seen enough water to float a boat (and he did it while surrounded by hostile and wicked neighbors). Steadfastness and perseverance require us to determinedly continue an action we know to be right even when we see little if any result.

In a business climate that honors aggressiveness, patience looks like insecurity. On the other hand, steadfastness can look like rigidity in an environment that glorifies flexibility and change. Ants are steadfast: destroy their anthill, and they get busy and rebuild it. Yet those who are steadfast in the biblical sense are not consumed by a task.

The testing of steadfastness in them girds their faith: "The testing of your faith produces steadfastness. And let steadfastness have its full effect, that you may be perfect and complete, lacking in nothing."[11] The psalmist testifies, "Because your steadfast love is better than life, my lips will praise you. So I will bless you as long as I live; in your name I will lift up my hands."[12]

PART IV
CAUTION AND ENCOURAGEMENT

In Part IV, we humbly offer caution for Christ-centered leaders in three challenging areas: (1) surrendering what can destroy, (2) character building, and (3) legalism. But throughout all three chapters, we also offer encouragement.

In conversation with a noted Christian business leader, I asked, "If you could assign a dollar figure to the investment of others' time and energy into your leadership development throughout the years, what would be the cost?"

"How can I estimate the cost?" he replied. "It's been priceless."

Caution and encouragement are both part of such investment. And so, in our effort to invest in you, please accept not only the cautions we offer but our encouragement as well.

CHAPTER SEVENTEEN

SURRENDER PRIDE, POWER-SEEKING, FEARFULNESS, AND UNRESOLVED ANGER

We have to do it if we want to develop as Christ-centered leaders—take a hard look at four areas that, if not surrendered, can destroy not only our leadership but our organization's culture.

PRIDE

For multiple reasons, pride is enemy number one in any organizational culture. Pride ruins relationships by elevating self, and both pride and arrogance result from valuating ourselves by our accomplishments or successes. Since I "did it myself," it's only logical to expect that the rewards are focused on me. Satisfaction can result in pride. In Hosea 13:6, God said, "When [the Israelites] were fed, they became satisfied; when they were satisfied, they became proud; as a result, they forgot me" (NET).

Our "will" becomes the deciding factor, yet though "the way of fools seem right to them . . . the wise listen to advice."[1] Even leaders not seeking to reflect Jesus recognize the dangers of pride. Attila the Hun said, "Seldom are self-centered, conceited and self-admiring chiefs great leaders, but they are great idolizers of themselves."[2] Pride is the highest form of idolatry. Even Attila the Hun understood that.

Pride separates us from God— "In his pride the wicked man does not seek him; in all his thoughts there is no room for God."[3] Prideful people lose track of their need for God and think they need to rely only on themselves to "improve" or "try harder." But God tells us He requires us to walk humbly with Him: "He has told you, O man, what is good; and what does the LORD require of you but to do justice, and to love kindness, and to walk humbly with your God?"[4]

God hates pride, and in the life of Nebuchadnezzar, we see what can happen when pride takes over:

> Now I, Nebuchadnezzar, praise and exalt and glorify the King of heaven, because everything he does is right, and all his ways are just. And those who walk in pride he is able to humble.[5]

But then,

> When [Nebuchadnezzar's] heart became arrogant and hardened with pride, he was deposed from his royal throne and stripped of his glory.[6]

Pride separates us from those we lead. Pride is self-promotion. Pride makes others feel we think we're in a different category, somehow better than they are. Even if we show them love, this causes a feeling of shame in the recipient. Because of our pride, they interpret love as condescension on our part.

Pride destroys trust. When a leader focuses on placing his position in the best light, sometimes even by minimizing others' contributions, fellow employees lose confidence and trust in that leader.

Pride blinds us to our faults. It makes us the center of our universe. This results in our filtering every event through our own eyes, and that's called narcissism. *How will this event make me appear in another's eye? Is it beneficial to my career or detrimental?* And remember, Jesus told us, "Why do you see the speck that is in your brother's eye, but do not notice the log that is in your own eye?"[7]

Pride makes others feel less safe or comfortable around us. They begin to wonder if, in the process of self-promotion, we will attack them to maintain our sense of self-importance. Will we be willing to protect them from outside threats? Or will we be willing to sacrifice them to defend ourselves?

Pride makes us unteachable. We are no longer willing to listen or be objective about others' ideas and solutions, all to the organization's detriment.

Pride exaggerates our need to be in control. If someone fails within our sphere of leadership, we become embarrassed. We don't want it to reoccur, so we attempt to take control by making rules or using force.

Pride has no limits. Money and status can encourage the growth of pride. One day Jesus was talking with the Pharisees and made a comment about this:

> "No servant can serve two masters, for either he will hate
> the one and love the other, or he will be devoted to the
> one and despise the other. You cannot serve God and

money." The Pharisees, who were lovers of money, heard all these things, and they ridiculed him.[8]

The Pharisees remained convinced that their money placed them at a higher status than Jesus's.

As leaders, how can we avoid becoming proud? By being thankful. It's challenging to be grateful when we're busy being prideful. Gratitude is an expression of thankfulness to God, and it's difficult to thank Him for what we have when we think we're the source of it all. We need to be careful when God blesses us. If we don't have a spirit of thankfulness, we can easily forget Him and become filled with pride.

Intentionally thank your followers and serve them by valuing each one and seeking their good fortune.

POWER-SEEKING

Are you more excited by the accumulation of power or by the empowerment of others? The first will crush; the other will build up. One creates wars; the other yields peace. One brings separation; the other brings unity. The pursuit of one is idolatry, for God alone has true power; the other turns recipients toward God.

The accumulation of power makes us power-full. Seeking power for power's sake is a selfish act. Power is the twin of pride. They go hand in hand, and like pride, power destroys trust and alienates potential followers. We need to remember that power opens us to the temptation of using it to serve ourselves. If we give in to the temptation of power and the urge to seek it, it destroys the trust our followers place in us.

Baron John Dalberg-Acton said,[9] "Power tends to corrupt, and absolute power corrupts absolutely. Great men are almost always bad men, even when they exercise influence and not authority, still more when you add the tendency or the certainty of corruption by authority."

Jesus is seated at the right hand of all Power.[10] But human power makes people feel like they're a god—harsh words for today when we spend so much of our effort trying to grasp the upper hand. Politics and power seem to go hand in hand. The desire for power blinds many and blurs our ethical concepts.

Lest we think this is a new phenomenon, Micah, in about 700 BC, wrote,

> The faithful have been swept from the land; not one upright person remains. Everyone lies in wait to shed blood; they hunt each other with nets. Both hands are skilled in doing evil; the ruler demands gifts, the judge accepts bribes, the powerful dictate what they desire— they all conspire together.[11]

FEARFULNESS

Fearfulness on the part of leaders negatively affects the culture within their organizations. Fear separates them from their followers and their associates. But why are some leaders so fearful?

Fear of Being Diminished

For a relatively brief time, I reported to someone who lived in fear of having to report bad news. Why? Because then people—and his superiors—would view him as a poor manager. This is the most challenging kind of leader to follow because they're subject to changing direction multiple times.

Victor needed to be a part of every meeting, even if it was highly technical and totally out of his range of expertise or experience.[12] And every decision required his approval. He was fearful a decision made without him would damage his reputation, keeping him from reaching success. He also wanted to ensure his manager knew he was active in making decisions (only the good ones, of course) so he could receive credit. He often made exaggerated promises to his manager that forced his team to work overtime.

At that time, I was a relative newbie to the world of large corporations, and one day Victor pulled me aside in the cafeteria to share some advice. "Jim," he essentially said, "to be successful here, you need a scapegoat for every project, so you'll have someone to blame if things go wrong. You also need to climb the ladder of success quickly so you'll already be promoted should the project develop severe problems. Then you'll no longer be directly associated with it, but your scapegoat will be."

Maybe you work with someone like that—someone who's always the first one in his manager's office in the morning and back again as everyone else is leaving. Victor lived in fear of being moved to a position in the organization that had less visibility. He feared being diminished.

Fear of Making the Wrong Decision

Some leaders fear making the wrong decision. Worse, when they ask for help or a recommendation, the last person they talk with is always right.

I worked for a leader who repeatedly vacillated this way. It was incredibly frustrating to hear that, after we agreed upon an action plan, he consulted with another manager and changed his mind. In one case, I had already signed a new contract with a vendor, which had to be canceled and caused our organization to lose money. It also placed financial hardship on the vendor and their employees.

As a leader, study an opportunity carefully and then stick with your decision. Otherwise, you'll soon become known as untrustworthy.

Fear of Vulnerability

Another barrier to a good relationship with your followers is the fear of vulnerability. Abraham struggled with this fear. When he found himself in King Abimelech's territory, he was afraid, so he lied by saying Sarah, his wife, was his sister. Earlier, Abraham had told a similar lie to Pharaoh. His son Isaac pulled the same stunt with Abimelech, claiming Rebekah, his wife, was his sister.[13, 14]

The fear of having to admit you don't know all the answers may cause you to avoid asking for help, believing your ability as a leader is in question. Here, false pride is fear in action.

Fear of Intimacy with Others

When you lose intimacy with God, and you distance yourself from His unconditional love, you fear intimacy with others. You, like a chicken, scratch up sand to make a cloud of dust to hide behind. You use all kinds of ways to place barriers around yourself to avoid the risk of exposing your fears. The isolation created by the fear of intimacy leaves leaders vulnerable to being blindsided by changing times and circumstances. When they operate under the constant threat of having their fear exposed, their anxiety spreads throughout the entire organization. And anxiety, having established roots, is challenging to eliminate.

How do we conquer these and other fears? By remembering we serve a faithful God interested only in our good. God is fully aware of every single need we have. Fear comes when we consider that we might not achieve our hopes. When facing fear, we need to be faithful to God and remember that His promises eliminate fear from our lives.

Once again, as Rick and I tell our stories in this book, we frequently refer to Paul's statement in Romans: "We know that for those who love God all things work together for good, for those who are called according to his purpose."[15] That's because God gave us this verse to provide us with hope and to help us conquer fear whenever we were faced with an opportunity to undertake a new challenge, so we wanted to show God's faithful working for our good through all the circumstances of our lives to encourage you in turn.

Hope in God's love casts out fear: "There is no fear in love, but perfect love casts out fear. For fear has to do with punishment, and whoever fears has not been perfected in love."[16] We live amid chaos, and only confidence in God's loyal love will enable us to keep our fears in proper perspective. Fear separates us from our followers, while shared hope builds relationships.

What happens when pride and fear exist side by side? Personal relationships dissolve, trust becomes paranoia, the feeling of safety and protection dissipate, our need to follow rules increases, and innovation and teachability are discouraged. Once pride and fear invade an organization, it usually dies. Or at best, it goes into hibernation.

UNRESOLVED ANGER

I had completely lost control.

Our biggest competitor had filed a lawsuit against DLP, Inc., for patent infringement, yet this competitor had built his business by copying our product and strategies.[17] He was so bold as to take photos of our products for his introductory literature and represent them as his.

I was angry beyond belief, and for three years, I let this fight consume me. I spent hundreds of thousands of dollars to prove that my anger was righteous indignation, and I was determined to control this situation.

Finally, to my discredit, my competitor made the first move. He called me and said, "Let's talk." We did, and in thirty minutes, we'd reached an agreement that cross-licensed our patents and both walked away relieved.

I had made two mistakes. First, I should have been the one to initiate that call. Second, I refused to humble myself and discontinue the "war" I'd been fighting not just with the person suing me but with God, all because I wanted to control the situation. My prayers for relief from the lawsuit went unanswered until my competitor humbled me by his actions.

My obsession with the lawsuit had a profoundly negative impact on my company, my family, and me. I've seen families and businesses split apart because of unresolved anger between individuals, the original cause often forgotten. Such unresolved anger interferes with our ability to worship Him.

God forgives sin, and He wants us to model forgiveness to the world. But He requires us first to forgive others so we can accept forgiveness. The consequences of harboring anger are disastrous, both physically and spiritually. As Christians, it's our responsibility to forgive even when the other person is unwilling to forgive us. The longer the anger continues, the harder it is to resolve.

Was this righteous anger? No, deep down, I knew my pride was the cause of my anger. God wants to unleash His power, and He will if we humble ourselves and ask Him to take control of the messes we make. Do we want to continue to pursue true justice or revenge?

Jesus said,

Come to terms quickly with your accuser while you are going with him to court, lest your accuser hand you over to the judge, and the judge to the guard, and you be put in prison. Truly, I say to you, you will never get out until you have paid the last penny.[18]

James wrote,

Know this, my beloved brothers: let every person be quick to hear, slow to speak, slow to anger; for the anger of man does not produce the righteousness of God.[19]

And Paul wrote,

Beloved, never avenge yourselves, but leave it to the wrath of God, for it is written, "Vengeance is mine, I will repay, says the Lord."[20]

Why all the Bible verses? Because I need reminders. When I think about that lawsuit, it still stirs up anger. I recently came across this saying, and I need to keep it in mind: "Holding on to anger makes as much sense as drinking poison and waiting for the other person to die."

The next chapter encourages you to address character issues in your own life—a challenge Rick and I support wholeheartedly.

CHAPTER EIGHTEEN

ADDRESS CHARACTER ISSUES

Sadly, many businesses and organizations endure leaders who demonstrate questionable character. But leadership without character formation is like building a castle on a stretch of sand—there's nothing to stand on when the storm winds blow, and the waters rise. Leaders not finishing well is often due to character defects, but Christ-centered leadership must be grounded in godly character.

If our leadership is to reflect Christ, we need to pursue the virtues described in Scripture.

From Colossians:

> Therefore, as God's chosen people, holy and dearly loved, clothe yourselves with compassion, kindness, humility, gentleness, and patience. Bear with each other and forgive one another if any of you has a grievance against someone. Forgive as the Lord forgave you. And over all virtues put on love, which binds them all together in perfect unity.[1]

And from 2 Peter:

Make every effort to supplement your faith with virtue, and virtue with knowledge, and knowledge with self-control, and self-control with steadfastness, and steadfastness with godliness, and godliness with brotherly affection, and brotherly affection with love. For if these qualities are yours and are increasing, they keep you from being ineffective or unfruitful in the knowledge of our Lord Jesus Christ. For whoever lacks these qualities is so nearsighted that he is blind, having forgotten that he was cleansed from his former sins.[2]

Let's take a brief look at the character virtues of compassion, kindness, humility, gentleness, and patience. You can find many good books that explain them in more detail, and they are applicable across all areas of life. However, our comments will focus on their application in the workplace. After that, we'll look at forgiveness, love, knowledge of the Lord, and self-control.

COMPASSION

Compassion is a characteristic of outstanding Christ-centered leadership, a confirmation that Christ's love is in us. Compassion is different from pity or feeling sorry for someone, and that's because it requires action. Compassion requires us to sacrifice; it always costs us something. Yet compassion is a gift freely offered, and we shouldn't expect anything in return.

Leadership is full of stress and frustration, but if we as leaders are focused on self, we can't show genuine compassion. It can be petty and cruel to hide behind a closed door because we don't want to hear about a follower's difficulty. We can't put ourselves first even though we're exhausted—or even angry.[3]

KINDNESS

Kindness is a virtue that magnifies the glory of God. Kindness grows, flows, and cascades in ever-increasing abundance. Kindness reflects His goodness everywhere. Kindness builds relationships, unites families and nations, and develops a pattern that can last through generations. God could not turn His back on Israel even though they had been unfaithful to Him. He continued to show them kindness.[4]

Followers treated with kindness are more willing to follow. Acts of kindness can become a daily way of living, of caring for whoever is in need. Simple gifts like helping your associate complete a task or switching your schedule to enable someone to enjoy a day off are meaningful acts of kindness.

Often leaders who show forgiveness and kindness may not be rewarded or even acknowledged for their integrity. Like infants taught to walk, our followers don't always remember the patience and kindness they received. However, kindness is usually reciprocal, building strong, lasting relationships. If you show kindness it will self-seed throughout your organization. The Lord delights in kindness:

> When the goodness and loving kindness of God our Savior appeared, he saved us, not because of works done by us in righteousness, but according to his own mercy, by the washing of regeneration and renewal of the Holy Spirit.[5]

HUMILITY

Although we've talked about humility previously, it's so essential to Christ-centered leadership that we need to discuss it further.

Humility is the most misunderstood virtue of the twenty-first century. We tend to think humility is the opposite of pride.

We associate it with weakness, poverty, the uneducated, and losers. But if not humility, what is pride's opposite? I would like to offer thankfulness and agape love for your consideration.

Humility knows God is all-sufficient: "When pride comes, then comes disgrace, but with the humble is wisdom."[6] Humbleness brings understanding. I know I learn much more and greatly benefit when I am humble.

If we study successful organizations that failed, we discover a time of pride, and an unteachable spirit preceded that failure. Shareholders who allowed or encouraged pride and self-importance in the organization's leadership lost millions of dollars. But humility brings wisdom to an organization's leaders. It keeps them teachable and opposes selfish ambition.[7] And besides, God hears those who come in humility.[8]

Humility in leadership brings the insight needed to succeed; bolsters growth by making us better listeners; guards against vanity, which creates division; lightens our load by putting God in charge; and dignifies our followers.

Humility is a required leadership quality if we are to lead well. It continually reminds us of who the ultimate leader is and why we need to follow Him. God is the epitome of humility because He waits for us to ask Him into our lives instead of barging in.

Humility is acknowledging God as our true leader and that we cannot lead without His guidance. The Bible tells us God talked with Moses face-to-face,[9] and that Moses was the humblest of all men.[10] There is a direct relationship between the two.

The more we understand God's greatness, the humbler we become. Self-worth does not come from our accomplishments but from the realization that we are created in the image of this awesome God. A spirit of thankfulness reminds us to be humble. Leaders model a spirit of humility and gratitude when they thank God and others for their success.

GENTLENESS

All leaders need to practice gentleness. Imagine you're in a hospital operating room watching a four-pound infant lying on an operating table with a blue cast because his blood isn't circulating correctly. The surgeon gently places a tiny stitch in a heart smaller than the end of your thumb. The sick heart begins beating strongly, and the blue cast disappears as the baby receives oxygenated blood. The tiny infant is gently healed.

Are we gentle healers for those who have failed? Or do we represent harshness to them? Do we condemn them with cutting words that carry exceptional weight because of our position as a leader, damaging them far into the future? Or are we gentle encouragers, whispering support and then coaching them on to victory by giving them another opportunity? Do we gently close our teammates' wounds? Do we reflect God to our team members by showing a gentle spirit?

Jesus rode peacefully into Jerusalem on a donkey.[11] God spoke to Elijah in a quiet whisper,[12] while a violent people drove God to the brink of destroying the earth.[13] A friend once took me up short by declaring that rushing is an act of violence! I thought I was a gentle person, but her statement made me think, and I had to agree with her insight. Rushing creates tension and leads to accidents. Rushing devalues relationships, makes us unwilling to listen, elevates us over others, robs us of the pleasure of the moment, and creates misunderstandings.

Aggressive leadership creates followers who fear and rebel. Gentle leadership creates followers who are loyal and kind.

God may need to get our attention in dramatic ways, but He often reveals Himself in unexpected ways, the quiet voice, or the gentlest touch. If Jesus was a gentle leader, shouldn't we be also? As a leader, you must be willing to comfort others gently. When someone fails after doing their very best, protect them from criticism and encourage them to move ahead again by ensuring them that willingness to take a risk comes with a reward.

Our gentleness comes from Jesus Christ, expresses itself in community, and has immense power to change others! We assume gentleness is not a force, yet a gently flowing stream has the power to cut through rock.

PATIENCE

Patience is the virtue of waiting despite our eagerness to move forward. Patience requires us to wait until someone else takes action. Giving God time to act also requires patience. God's grace works quietly and powerfully behind the scenes.

Forty days is an interesting length of time in the Bible—the length of time humankind could endure a trial. Jesus's testing in the wilderness lasted for forty days and forty nights. Paul received forty lashes less one five times. In the days of Noah, God sent what seemed like never-ending rain that lasted for forty days and nights. Moses spent forty years in Pharaoh's courts as a prince and then forty years as a shepherd, a job the Egyptians detested. That was followed by forty years leading the Israelites out of Egypt.

Yet we are impatient because, to us, forty days feels like forty years. But by being quiet before the Lord, we give Him time to demonstrate His grace. As leaders, we need to ensure that we don't rush ahead of our followers. Instead, we should graciously provide them with the necessary time to do a task the way they think is best. In doing so, we reflect God's grace and demonstrate our trust in them.

FORGIVENESS

Should you forgive that employee whose slackness just cost you a significant order, the competitor who repeatedly uses questionable tactics, or that partner who blew it?

Forgiveness isn't merely an emotion, although our first reaction is often to retaliate. But Jesus forgave without retaliation—and He forgave without waiting for repentance. Remember Peter? He denied the Lord three times just as Jesus had predicted. But after Christ's resurrection, He instructed the angel at the tomb to say these words: "Go, tell his disciples and Peter that he is going before you to Galilee. There you will see him, just as he told you."[14] Jesus not only forgave Peter before he could personally express repentance but later promoted him to a leadership position in the building of His kingdom!

Forgive honest failure. Demonstrate an attitude of grace, not legality. Prepare yourself to forgive and continue to trust those you lead. If you don't, you'll grow increasingly consumed by your anger and become an ineffective leader. One of the most effective ways to change a person's behavior is to forgive. Forgiveness heals rather than alienates a follower by gently making them aware of the correct action under the circumstances. In addition, forgiveness will strengthen you. Think of it as the power to act, an action under your control, a decision you can make.

If you're profoundly wounded, the process of forgiveness starts with your promise to forgive. Then as you continue to work toward forgiving, eventually, with God's help, you reach a point where it comes from your heart.

What happens if we don't forgive? Or if we wait for repentance or we withhold forgiveness even with it? We're tortured by our angry thoughts. Yes, the price of holding on to anger is torture. Holding on to it consumes us. It eats up everything and everyone around us. Remember my story about angrily fighting an injustice for three years, to the detriment of my family, my business, and even to me.

Jesus taught that forgiveness has no limit, asking us to forgive as many times as we are wronged: "If your brother sins, rebuke him, and if he repents, forgive him, and if he sins against you seven times in the day, and turns to you seven times, saying, 'I repent,' you must forgive him."[15] That kind of forgiveness forces us to confront our anger and impatience.

Of course, God not only forgives our sins but is more than willing to forget them. The Bible repeatedly tells us this is the case.[16] If we were required to suffer daily for our sin, could we focus on worshipping Him? Would we feel worthy and like an honorable member of His family? Or would we always think we needed to prove our worth or feel second-class?

If we want to develop capable and healthy followers, if we want them to remain a part of our team, we must not only forgive their offenses but put them aside and move on.

LOVE

First Corinthians tells us what love is and isn't:

> Love is patient and kind; love does not envy or boast; it is not arrogant or rude. It does not insist on its own way; it is not irritable or resentful; it does not rejoice at wrongdoing, but rejoices with the truth. Love bears all things, believes all things, hopes all things, endures all things.[17]

Love is the motivating force God's kingdom is based on:

> A new commandment I give to you, that you love one another: just as I have loved you, you also are to love one another. By this all people will know that you are my disciples, if you have love for one another.[18]

Christ said His followers would be recognized by their love. This is His command, not our choice, and obeying it is necessary. You can't love others and at the same time believe you're in an elevated position in comparison. Jesus warned against this:

Beware of the scribes, who like to walk around in long robes, and love greetings in the marketplaces and the best seats in the synagogues and the places of honor at feasts, who devour widows' houses and for a pretense make long prayers. They will receive the greater condemnation.[19]

And so loving as leaders is not about thinking solely of ourselves but about daily taking personal interest in our followers and considering what's best for them, not just what's best for us or for our firms.

KNOWLEDGE OF THE LORD

According to God's Word, knowledge of the Lord is available to everyone: "The earth will be filled with the knowledge of the glory of the LORD as the waters cover the sea."[20] Deepening our knowledge of the Lord is necessary if we want to grow in faith. Such knowledge is less about books, computers, the internet, and Google, rather it is experiencing God at work in our lives. People who seek to add to their knowledge of the Lord by diligent study of his word will also experience new and challenging opportunities that work together to increase their faith and wisdom.

Every good leader teaches—not just giving information but imparting knowledge. To do that as Christ-centered leaders, we require wisdom from God. The Bible tells us, "If any of you lacks wisdom, let him ask God, who gives generously to all without reproach, and it will be given him."[21]

Gaining knowledge of the Lord is crucial not only through His church but in the workplace.

SELF-CONTROL

Self-control is necessary for leaders, but it's also a healthy lifestyle. In the following passage, Paul provides a prescription for a healthy lifestyle that puts us squarely on the road to winning that imperishable crown.

> Do you not know that in a race all the runners run, but only one receives the prize? So run that you may obtain it. Every athlete exercises self-control in all things. They do it to receive a perishable wreath, but we an imperishable. So I do not run aimlessly; I do not box as one beating the air.

Self-control is necessary for not only a balanced life but to ready us for the work God has set before us. It's easy to mistake following a set of rules for self-control, but it works the other way around. Legalism replaces our self-control. (It also stunts growth and faith, the subject of our next chapter.)

In our walk as followers of Christ, we need to vigorously oppose all efforts that distract from our goal of living our lives for the glory of God. In the workplace, we should ensure that we maintain a steady direction so others can follow.

CHAPTER NINETEEN

UNDERSTAND WHAT LEGALISM CAN DO

Legalism is the strict adherence to law or prescription, especially to the letter of the law rather than the spirit of the law. Because of our human nature, we often find it easier to revert to following a set of rules than to make our own decisions. And leaders, for various reasons, can put legalism into play, stunting the growth of their organizations and the growth of their followers.

Leaders may establish rules out of fear of being wrong or because they want to check off a list of things they've done to prove they're accomplished. But even more dangerous is the belief that they can use rules to ensure correct action instead of placing trust in their associates.

Using rules to control our followers is what Jesus was referring to when He said,

> Woe to you, scribes and Pharisees, hypocrites! For you tithe mint and dill and cumin, and have neglected the weightier matters of the law: justice and mercy and

faithfulness. These you ought to have done, without neglecting the others. You blind guides, straining out a gnat and swallowing a camel![1]

The scribes and Pharisees were the religious leaders of the people in Jesus's time. He saw them leading the people away from God with a legalistic attitude that had replaced relationship with the Lord. Laws outweighed grace in their guidebook. The Pharisees argued with Jesus about what was lawful to do on the Sabbath even to the point where they accused His disciples of working when they picked a few kernels of grain to eat as they walked through a field on the Sabbath.

Because of societies' mistaken belief that laws alone will keep someone from acting incorrectly or curbing someone's greed, we've also developed the *There ought to be a law* mentality. Publicity about the financial rewards given to leaders who skirt the law, for instance, has accelerated a perceived need for more control while missing the deceitfulness of man's heart.[2]

LEGALISM FROM THE OUTSIDE

Legalism can affect business from the outside as well. I had asked Vern Ehlers, our Michigan district's representative to the U.S. House at the time, to take a plant tour of DLP, Inc. After the tour, he asked me how he, as our representative, could help small businesses.

I replied, "The number of bills a legislator has successfully introduced appears to be a measure of their success when they come up for reelection, and consequently, we have to meet thousands of government regulations. At DLP, we try to comply with them. However, as I sit here talking with you, I'm probably violating at least a hundred or more rules I don't even know about or have time to find."

LEGALISM AFFECTS CUSTOMERS AND CLIENTS

Earl Backen, the founder of Medtronic, created a great picture for his corporate vice presidents at an annual strategic planning retreat. After completing the day's schedule, they were all relaxing in the lodge around a roaring fire when Earl entered the room with several large, standard operating procedure manuals chained to his leg. He hobbled up to the fire, then pulled up a chair, and without uttering a word, began ripping out the pages and throwing them into the fire.

Earl was showing the vice presidents that, in his opinion, standards and policies were multiplying so fast that they were beginning to interfere with the company's ability to help the customer "toward a full life," their mission statement. They were replacing training and trust with legalistic procedures.

The group had to sit quietly for an "eternity" until the manuals were empty, but they got the message.

Legalism vs. Empowerment

As leaders, we need procedures for guidance, but total reliance on them, believing they're sufficient, should never be allowed. Imagine that Sarah, a new employee, has just joined your team. Initially, you give her guidelines to follow when completing a specific task. When she does something incorrectly, you show her grace by carefully explaining what went wrong and how to correct it.

As Sarah becomes more proficient and performs well, you allow her to make minor decisions by removing some of the rules. A trust relationship begins to build between Sarah, the others on the team, and you as the leader. You continue to empower Sarah by giving her the authority to make decisions, and this authority gives her more responsibility, freedom to work to the best of her ability, and job satisfaction.

Unfortunately, not all managers lead with empowerment. Some hold tight to legalism, to the rules they create or at least embrace.

LEGALISM IS DETRIMENTAL TO ORGANIZATIONS

Imagine a young company that's rapidly growing. Jack's department has performed exceptionally well and kept up with the growth. He's proud of how his department has responded, and he believes they've been able to perform well because he's made the right decisions. In fact, no one else is allowed to make decisions. He's also set the rules, and they're to be followed.

But now so many people in his department are coming to him for decisions that he can no longer keep up with the volume, and the performance of his department begins to decline. Not only that, but this rule-following culture Jack created spreads across the organization. Its entire culture becomes toxic. Everything and everyone outside the organization is blamed for the organization's condition when the real cause is leaders demanding their subordinates follow the rules rather than empowering them. If allowed to continue, the organization will eventually cease to exist.

Building a culture simultaneously with the establishment of a new organization is crucial, and as I've said, we were able to do that with DLP, Inc. But if an organization substitutes rules to avoid empowering individuals or in place of competent managers, its death becomes a distinct possibility. The difference between legalism and empowerment is that legalism results in death and empowerment results in growth.

As an organization grows, it needs to expand. It needs to efficiently change to meet the requirements created by its growth. Leaders have two choices: attempt to remain in control by issuing detailed directions and rules on how to handle a specific activity or empower people to make decisions and let them help the organization.

Instead, the desire to control outcomes results in a spirit of legalism that creates attitudes like *It's not my job*. And if the leaders stand by and allow their managers to create a culture where rules outweigh reason, the organization becomes legalistic, rigid, and ceases to grow and even begins to decline.

There's an inward focus while ignoring events and developments outside of the organization that may negatively affect it. And when the leaders in an organization look only at their organization's performance as a "benchmark," they can become self-confident. This type of evaluation leads to a state of "satisfactory underperformance."[3] Leaders must look outward and forward, not backward and down when evaluating their organization's performance.

To remain healthy, an organization needs to continually renew itself. The authentic leader does not seek power. He or she instead wants to share their "power" by empowering others. Authentic leaders understand their abilities and shortcomings. They lead with integrity and value long-term relationships, not rules.

Legalism is so dangerous it can kill an organization. And how does it affect people from a spiritual perspective? The short answer is it stunts faith and makes grace inoperative. Perhaps that's the worst outcome of all.

CLOSING THOUGHTS

Thank you for investing your time in reading this book. Perhaps our stories have resonated with you, knowing we've struggled with some of the same challenges that challenge you. But our stories don't stop there. They show God actively weaving His golden thread throughout our lives, proving that "for those who love God all things work together for good, for those who are called according to his purpose."[1] And with that, we hope we've encouraged you.

We also hope we've illustrated that Christ-centered leadership requires an absolute commitment to the values of Jesus Christ. We all have failings and shortfalls, and in casual conversation, I often use the illustration of God using a plank to knock off my sharp corners and rough edges because I remain a work in progress. Still, the gifts God has given me enable me to serve Him. The gifts He's given you enable you to do the same.

Remember, it's who you are, not what you do, that most conveys the gospel to others. They will be attracted to the good news not by any attempted portrait of perfection but by your authenticity. By placing *you* in your workplace, even with your sharp corners and rough edges, God creates multiple opportunities for you to touch lives and touch them deeply. A rushing waterfall is beautiful, but a constant and quiet stream carves its way through the countryside, nourishing and supporting a whole host of God's creation.

The book of Psalms begins,

> Blessed is the man who walks not in the counsel of the wicked, nor stands in the way of sinners, nor sits in the seat of scoffers; but his delight is in the law of the LORD, and on his law he meditates day and night. He is like a tree planted by streams of water that yields its fruit in its season, and its leaf does not wither. In all that he does, he prospers.[2]

As I said at the beginning, we wanted this book to help you be a more effective leader, reflecting Christ all along the way; understand that the focus of your leadership must be upward toward God and outward toward others; and make a significant, positive impact on those God gives you to lead. May it be so as again I share this passage:

The LORD bless you and keep you; the LORD make his face to shine upon you and be gracious to you; the LORD lift up his countenance upon you and give you peace.[3]

LEARNING TO COMMUNICATE RESPONSIBLY[1]

RICK SESSOMS

I got acquainted with Peter while pastoring a church outside New York City in the early 1990s. He and his wife, Carolyn, attended the church and dutifully listened to my weekly sermons.

Peter and I had breakfast together every other week and played golf as often as we could, and those were the moments when I would ask for his help with my latest ministry challenges. He was a well-paid communications coach for Manhattan executives, so I felt privileged to have him as my confidant.

In those days, as a young and ambitious pastor, I was determined to grow the church. I boldly introduced new approaches that attracted many newcomers, but conflict was ever-present with some established parishioners. Congregational meetings became highly charged as I often exerted a firm hand to ensure that the church stayed on course with our plan. Tension mounted.

On one fateful morning, Peter and I were in our usual corner of the café we frequented, enjoying coffee and muffins. I asked him what he thought was going wrong in the church and to suggest what I could do to address the increasing strain.

"Rick, you speak pretty well and you're a forceful leader," he replied. "But you consistently seem to want to top what people have to say, to prove something to them. You're like a bull trying to dominate the herd. You're a poor listener."

I had assumed Peter would take my side and say that others were the problem, so naturally his answer felt like a sharp blow. Later that day, wanting to test his analysis, I asked my wife if she thought I was a poor listener.

"Honey, I love you," Tina responded kindly, "but yes, you're a lousy listener."

That was not what I wanted to hear, and it was not a view of myself I cherished—argumentative, bullheaded, trampling on other people. It was hard to accept, but I had to consider the input seriously since both Peter and Tina said it was so. I was faced directly with a contradiction between what I believed about myself and what others saw in me. It was like living in a hall of mirrors: there was no hiding from the reflections they gave me.

Two weeks later, I met with Peter again. I told him about the conversation with Tina and expressed my need for help to become a better listener. I'm grateful that, instead of turning me away, Peter said he'd help.

For the next two years, Peter gave me challenging assignments to improve my listening, and I could always trust him to support me and provide honest feedback about my progress. Sometimes he complimented me for exhibiting good listening in a public setting, and other times he pointed out ways I could listen better. The journey was sometimes quite tricky, but ultimately it was transformational.

Today Tina assures me I am a better listener (although I still have occasional lapses), and the impact on my leading others has been encouraging. I'd like to share with you some of the communication tools I've learned over the years—for both responsible listening and responsible speaking.

RESPONSIBLE LISTENING

The most powerful communication tool at a leader's disposal is listening. We communicate well when we listen well.

The reverse plays out often, and most of us have experienced it. You meet someone at a conference, let's say a man. As you read his name badge, you engage him in friendly conversation: "Hello, Harry, what do you do?" Five minutes later, Harry hasn't stopped for breath! When he finally allows you to get in a word, he checks his watch, distracted. Harry has demonstrated no interest in you at all, and you have the urge to escape this awkward exchange.

If Harry had engaged with you in return—showing interest through dialogue—you would have a different opinion of him entirely.

Often listening is complex and challenging. Many barriers can cause us not to listen well. Here are a few:

SELECTIVE INTERPRETATION

When you're in conversation, you subconsciously interpret what the person is saying through your own experiences, preferences, knowledge, and opinions. Often these filters block the full message the other person is trying to convey.

FAMILIARITY

The better you know the other person in the conversation, the more difficult it is to listen well. For example, it's easier for me to listen to a stranger than to listen to my children. I have a history with my children, so I tend to predict what they'll say based on our history together. However, this temptation to predict what the other person is about to say shuts down my capacity to hear the complete message.

EMOTIONS

When the emotional level in a conversation goes up, the ability to listen well goes down.

FEAR OF CHANGE

Often leaders don't listen out of fear that the speaker's ideas or opinions may change their or others' thinking.

THE 600-WORD GAP

Researchers have shown we can comprehend words spoken at a rate of 750 words a minute. But people speak at an average rate of 150 words a minute. That makes a 600-word gap between the speed at which we can hear and the rate at which another person speaks to us.

This "gap" creates an opportunity for you to engage in a myriad of thoughts while listening. You think about lunch, the argument with your spouse, or the report you need to write. More likely, you're also formulating your responses to the other person as they speak. Unfortunately, all these mental activities taking place during the other person's speech cause you to not listen well.

Peter taught me that, when we listen responsibly, we commit ourselves to proving to the other person that we've heard the full message they want to convey. When in a conversation, the other person wants to know we've listened to what they've said.

So how do you prove to someone that you're listening? You provide them with evidence that you've understood what they've said. You reflect on what they've told you by restating it for clarification or asking questions that develop the theme and extend the information shared.

Give responsible listening a try and see what happens. In your next conversation, practice this feedback loop with the other person:

- Ask questions.
- Clarify what you understood.
- Adapt what you say to meet their need as they related it.

On one occasion, I was teaching responsible communication to a group in which there was a newlywed. It seems that his new wife was always saying, "You don't listen to me." After sitting through the first day's session, he phoned his wife that night and there and then practiced the listening and feedback skills he'd learned.

In the next day's session, he reported that his wife said, "What are you doing in that seminar? You seem to be listening to me in a way you've never done before."

Responsible listening enables you to establish rapport with the people with whom you seek to communicate. It proves to them that you care. You demonstrate that they are essential. People appreciate and respond to a good listener. Being listened to and being loved are so close that most people can't tell the difference.

Here are two Scriptures that speak to responsible listening:

Let each of you look not only to his own interests, but also to the interests of others.[2]

Do not judge, or you too will be judged. For in the same way you judge others, you will be judged, and with the measure you use, it will be measured to you.[3]

RESPONSIBLE SPEAKING

If responsible listening is proving to others you've heard their full message, then responsible speaking is about taking responsibility for your listeners to listen and understand what you say.

Frank cornered his boss in a "conversation" at the coffee station. Because the boss couldn't easily escape, Frank took the opportunity to say a great deal he wanted to say, overwhelming him with information. Of course, Frank wasn't getting anywhere with his insensitive, one-sided communication style that ignored his listener's needs.

I hope I'm not as disrespectful as Frank was with his boss, but sometimes I've been just as ineffective in communicating with others.

Christ-centered leaders are committed to enabling others to achieve their full potential, and central to this focus is responsible speaking. We need to share ideas, objectives, and methods effectively.

Most leaders can speak well, but this does not guarantee that real communication is taking place. In the 1970s, Finnish professor Osmo Antero Wiio stated several "laws" of communication. Here are four of them:

- If communication can fail, it will.
- If a message can be interpreted in several ways, it will be interpreted in a manner that maximizes the damage.
- There is always someone who knows better than you what you meant with your message.
- The more we communicate, the worse communication succeeds.

These indicate that effective communication is enormously challenging; it doesn't just happen. And speaking well takes both an awareness of barriers that prevent listening and practice to overcome them, whether the conversation is one-to-one or one-to-many.

FIVE MISTAKES

Following are five mistakes leaders make when speaking that create barriers to understanding. They reflect some of what Professor Wiio was trying to say.

1. Overwhelming the listener with words

Like Frank, leaders are often so focused that they spew out words like automatic rifle fire. Sometimes they do it because they're short of time, but either way, the leader often overwhelms the listener, with the result that the listener doesn't understand the message. Under these circumstances, the leader can think, *I told them what they need to know!* But communication didn't happen.

What takes place within an overwhelmed listener? They don't have time to gather their thoughts, nor can they find a way to get more information or ask for help in understanding. This is a one-way conversation, and the longer the conversation flows in one direction, the less relevant the message becomes to the listener. When this happens, the leader's frustration can increase, and their typical reaction is to intensify their speaking.

Unfortunately, this approach usually eliminates any chance of healthy feedback. This kind of communication is similar to a PA system's painful feedback picked up by the microphone and amplified, emerging from the speaker only to be picked up and amplified more. The cycle keeps going until somebody turns down the volume.

How do we prevent overwhelming others? Think quality, not quantity. People can take in only so much information at a time. Think out what your listener needs to know and limit what you say.

Avoid being in a rush. Make sure you have time to help your listener understand. Allow your listener to ask questions.

2. Speaking only about what interests us, not the listener

How can you speak to create a path via the listener's interest so that understanding, and an appropriate response, take place? Whatever you're talking about, your listeners will have perspectives, concerns, objections, or insights on the matters that are important to them. The key to engaging them is finding out what's important to them and addressing those issues.

Whenever you're in a conversation, realize that the other person is continuously asking themselves a primary question: *What's in this message for me?*

An inner antenna is always filtering messages based on the benefit of the news to the listener. To motivate good listening, you must communicate a benefit for the listener if you want your message to affect them. If your message has no perceived value for them, they may be polite, especially if you're the boss, and then soon forget the message.

Most people invest their time to listen when they anticipate some kind of benefit, even if it's merely being able to follow instructions sufficiently well to do a good job. You can avoid their forgetting what you say by adapting what you say so your message addresses the other's needs. In a team situation, make sure to explain the information you provide clearly, so the team understands what actions are required.

3. Ignoring communication markers

Communication markers are the non-verbal cues the listener gives when you're speaking. In face-to-face conversations, these markers are primarily body language and facial expressions. They provide many insights into what your listener is thinking. Being sensitive to the markers will help you steer a course that keeps them engaged.

Remember Frank? He demonstrated a severe lack of sensitivity when he trapped his boss to get his attention. Unfortunately, when the boss backed up to the wall, folded his arms, and kept looking at his watch, Frank ignored the communication markers. He missed the obvious signals that said, *I've had enough; I need to go now.* How do we correct for missing the communication markers?

- Demonstrate concern for the other person. Do your utmost to make them feel an essential part of the conversation.
- Learn the physical signals. Some excellent resources can help you understand body language, but some of it is obvious. You won't miss it if you maintain your awareness of the other person.
- Listen for verbal cues. Communications markers are verbal as well as physical. Listen to changes in tone or message signals.

4. Assuming your listener understands you

If a leader "dumps" a message and then rushes off, it's easy for the leader to assume the listener has understood the message. But understanding is prevented for many reasons. Your listeners always have other things going on, so they're hearing through filters that can cause them to not tune in or to miss the point. Factors that may further obscure understanding are abstract concepts and the leader's attempt to be diplomatic.

Several years ago, I provided an evaluation process for a leader. In one session, he asked me to give him feedback on some leadership deficiencies that surfaced in his evaluation. I attempted to be diplomatic in my counsel. Then weeks later, I learned he interpreted my attempt at diplomacy as a compliment to his leadership style rather than counsel for change. I assumed he'd understood, and that was a costly mistake.

Communicating across cultures requires extra caution in our assumptions that messages are understood. We may be speaking with people for whom our language is not their first language. Issues of vocabulary and cultural implications can impede our attempts to communicate. Whatever the reason, the possibility that others don't fully understand what we've said exists. The consequence can be a misunderstanding, confusion, and even conflict. How do we correct this?

- Keep it simple. Use plain language and avoid jargon and idioms that assume knowledge on the part of the listener.
- Make space for understanding. Speak in shorter segments so the listener can assimilate what is said before you move on to the next idea.

5. *Making the listener responsible for understanding*

If they don't understand, they should ask may seem like a sensible thought, but it has at least two flaws. First, people tend not to ask leaders questions about what was just said out of fear of looking silly or perhaps because they fear the leader. Second, listeners often don't realize they don't understand. Most people attach their interpretation to what makes the most sense to them. But their understanding is often quite different from the leader's intended message.

When the message we intend to communicate seems clear to us, it can be difficult to appreciate that people may not have understood. After all, it's so apparent, isn't it? Furthermore, leaders may not feel it's their job to make sure their listeners understand. However, remember that it benefits both you and the listener when they know what you're saying. How do we correct this?

- Make understanding your goal. Measure effective communication based on whether the other person understands and can act accordingly.

- Avoid assumptions. Many actions fail due to assumptions. Recognize your natural assumptions, declare them, and test them with your listener.
- Partner with your listener. Communication succeeds only when both the speaker and the listener allow understanding to flow. Encourage your listener to participate in that partnership. Be aware that they need the leader's permission to join in.

Think of the people with whom you communicate regularly. Having achieved a level of rapport through responsible listening and speaking, communication becomes enjoyable. It moves from monologue to dialogue into an energized conversation. Information will be voluntarily shared, and comments will be shaped and purposed to meet each other's needs.

LEARNING FROM JESUS, THE MASTER COMMUNICATOR

MICHELLE SESSOMS

When we encounter Jesus in the New Testament, we tend to view Him as our Savior and Lord, the long-awaited Promised One. But how often do we view Him as the master communicator He was?

An Indian leader recently made this challenge when Freedom Lead International met with twenty-five ministry colleagues from India and Nepal to make plans for the first-ever Orality Institute of Leadership (OIL).[1]

These men and women will serve as certified facilitators in the Institute's regional hubs across this region. Students who attend this Institute will receive training and mentoring in character formation, biblical literacy, and ministry skills. And the unique curriculum will be entirely oral-based rather than literacy-based. The OIL is a historic initiative, the first of its kind. They will learn how to lead people effectively with Jesus as their ultimate model.

So let's go back to the challenge posed to us by our Indian brother. If we want to lead effectively with Jesus as our ultimate model, how did Jesus communicate? In collaboration with our Indian colleagues, we identified six different communication styles Jesus used.

JESUS TOLD GOOD STORIES

Luke told this story in chapter 7 of his Gospel. When Jesus ate at the house of Simon the Pharisee, a "woman of the city" (verse 37) came and anointed His feet with perfume and wiped them with her hair. Simon reacted as any good Pharisee would respond. I mean, imagine how you, a good Christian, might react if the same thing happened in your home with an honored guest and a "sinful woman." But let's not be too harsh on Simon here, because he could be any of us.

Jesus then used this opportunity to speak into Simon's life. But rather than lecture him, He told Simon a story about a moneylender with two debtors. One owed more than the other. He then canceled both of their debts. Jesus then asked questions. Upon Simon's answers, Jesus offered feedback and affirmation, pointing to the real-life example of the woman in front of Him to address the problem of the forgiveness of sins.

In this way, Simon might have been able to self-discover the truth more efficiently than by being told or directed. The mental images depicted through the story would more likely impact Simon's thinking and attitudes. Jesus had compassion for not only the "woman of the city," but He also had understanding for Simon by the way He respectfully communicated with him. Let's turn the tables for a minute. What do you think would have happened if Jesus had lectured Simon the Pharisee or given him a sermon?

When God chose to communicate with His people, He spoke through a Person. And this Person communicated through good stories. Seventy-five percent of the Bible is story. The New Testament epistles reinforce the stories in the Gospels, and even Peter and

Paul used the narrative of the Scriptures when they shared in the synagogues and the city squares throughout the Roman Empire.

We also shouldn't miss the point of why the stories were told. Jesus often spoke in parables not to tell a cute little story but for the sake of teaching the people. He created stories to bring heavenly meaning. The words themselves carried the truth.

JESUS USED EVERYDAY OBJECTS AND VERBAL IMAGERY

When Jesus talked about paying taxes to Caesar, He used an actual coin.[2] As usual, the Pharisees were on a mission to "entangle" Him using the current political situation. Being under Caesar's rule, they tried to get Jesus to say they should not pay taxes to Caesar. However, this would be an action against Roman law.

But rather than get riled up about the question, as the Pharisees expected Him to do, Jesus simply took an everyday object, the denarius coin, and He used it for this conversation as told in Matthew 22:

"Whose likeness and inscription is this?"

"Caesar's."

"Therefore render to Caesar the things that are Caesar's, and to God the things that are God's."

Jesus knew what was in the hearts of the Pharisees, and He used their example to turn it around on them.

Now, Jesus could have lectured. He could have filled his instructions with *oughts* and *musts* and *shoulds*. He could have delivered an hour-long sermon about the duty toward the state and responsibility toward God but didn't. He used a simple object and asked a simple question. The best part, though? "When they heard it, they marveled. And they left him and went away."[3]

In other situations, Jesus used vivid verbal imagery to illustrate what He was saying. Our Indian brother described it this way:

When you give people a mental picture, they will take it home, and it will be in their hearts for a long time. Jesus understood that. For example, when talking about the greatest in the kingdom of heaven, he said,

> Whoever receives one such child in my name receives me, but whoever causes one of these little ones who believe in me to sin, it would be better for him to have a great millstone fastened around his neck and to be drowned in the depth of the sea.[4]

I don't know what you imagine as Jesus describes that picture, but I see a millstone more massive than anything I could bear tied around my neck and then thrown into the sea as not exactly subtle. Granted, I don't use a millstone every day, but the people with Jesus did. Perhaps if He were telling this story today, He'd talk about tying a Volkswagen around one's neck and being thrown into the middle of one of the Great Lakes. That's certainly not an image we're likely to forget.

Jesus spoke in images, not abstract concepts. Whether peaceful pictures like flowers, birds of the air, mustard seeds, rocks, or more vivid images like millstones and the cutting off of hands, Jesus was always painting a mental image or picture.

JESUS ASKED GOOD QUESTIONS

Not only did Jesus tell good stories and use images, but He also asked good questions. He was involving the audience and getting them to realize they could discover the truth for themselves by asking them questions. There is power in self-discovery because it allows people to experience a new level of understanding.

Luke records Jesus asking His disciples this question: "Who do the crowds say that I am?"[5] Indeed, He knew the answer, but the disciples responded with, "John the Baptist. But others say, Elijah, and others, that one of the prophets of old has risen."[6]

At this point, Jesus could have said, "No, I am the Christ, the Son of the Living God." But instead, He asked another question: "Who do you say that I am?" Using this opportunity, Peter made one of the most significant declarations in Scripture: "The Christ of God!"[7]

A good Bible study exercise would be to print out the Gospel narratives and highlight all the places Jesus asked good questions. Here are just a few:

- To Peter, for the second time: "Simon, son of John, do you love me?" (John 21:16)
- To two blind men: "What do you want me to do for you?" (Matthew 20:32)
- To the bleeding woman: "Who was it that touched me?" (Luke 8:45)

Also see Matthew 7:3, 9:28, 12:11, 15:34; Mark 2:8, 10:3; Luke 10:36, 14:31, 17:18, 22:27; and John 5:6.

Just like He chose His stories, Jesus chose these questions carefully. He asked questions to teach people and to draw out the truth.

JESUS RELATED TRUTH TO REAL LIFE

As we interact with the way Jesus communicated as a model for us all, one question comes to mind: if His communication style was telling relevant stories and asking the right questions, what do we do with the Sermon on the Mount found in Matthew 5–7?

This is a valid question, especially when we see the word *sermon* in many Bible translations. Some may use this as evidence of focusing primarily on using good sermons and lecturing. However, when we look at the passage more closely, we see that the way Jesus "preached" was not the traditional ways we often preach in pulpits today.

In his Sermon on the Mount, Jesus used components that are common to life with standard themes and topics. He addressed practical issues: being salt and light, anger, lust, divorce, taking oaths, revenge, love for enemies. Also, giving, how to pray, fasting, anxiousness, judging, the Golden Rule, and fruitful living. He addressed the real needs of the people. And Jesus knew their needs because He'd spent time with them, asked them questions, listened to them, and ate with them.

In his book *Cross-Cultural Servanthood: Serving the World in Christlike Humility*, Duane Elmer says,

> I am disturbed by leaders who isolate themselves in their study for most of the week, spending little time being with people, and then deliver exegetically correct and rhetorically powerful sermons that are irrelevant to the person in the pew. The same is true for organizational leaders who are preoccupied with conferences, trips, and "important" meetings but who rarely take time to listen to their employees.[8]

In His Sermon on the Mount, Jesus employed the use of words, pictures, and imagery. He used language the people could understand in a way that wasn't offending. And when He wrapped up with the image of the wise and foolish builder, He was demonstrating again, through that story, that merely teaching without application is useless. Jesus spoke to them, and whatever the people heard, they were to apply to their lives.

If we look at the Sermon on the Mount again through this lens, what do we see differently now? Is it a sermon by our current definition?

JESUS SPOKE THE "PEOPLE'S LANGUAGE"

Think about the language Jesus used in different locations. To illustrate, let's look at three stories: His interaction with Nicodemus, the woman at the well, and the apostle Peter.

In John 3, He met Nicodemus. Speaking with a Pharisee familiar with the ways of the law and "ruler of the Jews," Jesus spoke at the man's education level. He used theological terms, like *born again*, the *kingdom of God*, *eternal life*, and the *light in the darkness*. He talked about Moses lifting up the serpent in the wilderness and comparing that with the lifting up of the Son of Man.

He also went directly to the point. Today we tend to zero in on a specific verse like John 3:16 and have our children memorize it: "For God so loved the world," it says. This verse is a continuation of Jesus's discussion with Nicodemus. He's still talking to Nicodemus using Nicodemus's language, not talking with children.

Now contrast that with Jesus's words to the woman at the well, a story told in John 4. Unusual for a Jewish man, Jesus identified with her, even though first, she was a woman; second, she was a Samaritan; and third, she'd had five husbands and was currently living with a sixth man. All three of those things would have given Jesus ample reason to stay away from her.

But He didn't. He used a simple way of connecting with her by identifying her need for Living Water. He could hear her desire for an encounter with the Messiah she didn't fully understand, but somehow she knew she was supposed to wait for Him. He didn't "dumb it down"; He just used a different language.

If Jesus had talked to the woman at the well the same way He spoke to Nicodemus, using a phrase like *You must be born again to receive eternal life*, how might that have registered with her, if at all? She might have thought, *Eternal life? Born again? What do those even mean? How is this good news for my present mess of a life?* At least, that's how I imagine she would've reacted. But Jesus chose to connect with her on a personal level, and her life was changed.

When Jesus called Peter to follow Him in Luke 5, He talked as one among fishermen. Jesus used the language of vinedressers and shepherds. He used language as a tool to bridge the gap to make healthy relationships.

However, it wasn't just about the words He used; it was also about language choice. Greek was the language of the Romans and many of the Jews in Jerusalem. Scripture was written in Hebrew. Jesus spent much of His ministry with people in Galilee, where Aramaic was the language. At any point in time, the trilingual Jesus adapted His speech to the culture.

When people don't understand our language, we tend to repeat the words, only louder and more dramatically. If they still don't understand, we tend to conclude they've hardened their hearts and refuse to listen. But could it be possible that the language we use, whether from behind the pulpit or face-to-face, is not communicating? How can we apply what we can learn from Jesus in this type of situation?

JESUS OFTEN SUMMARIZED STORIES

Jesus understood that He was talking with an oral-based, story-centric audience. With that kind of group, telling stories usually has one of two purposes: first, so these stories can be passed on to others or second, for the sake of transferring knowledge or information.

For example, when telling a Bible story for reproduction, accuracy needs to be maintained for oral audiences. That's why it's essential to tell biblical stories exactly how they are (and translated) in the Bible. However, in some cases, summarizing a narrative helps provide background knowledge. Jesus demonstrated this well with the story that takes place on the road to Emmaus.

After Jesus's resurrection, two disciples were walking along that road. Before recognizing the resurrected Jesus was the man walking beside them, they felt discouraged and explained to Him all that had happened that week. They told this stranger it had been filled with beatings and crucifixions and burials and women telling weird stories about empty tombs with angel visions. Then, when Jesus knew it was time to reveal Himself, "beginning with Moses and all the Prophets, he interpreted to them in all the Scriptures the things concerning himself."[9]

Now, I'm making a guess here because I wasn't there, but I think it would be safe to assume that Jesus didn't tell the entire story of Moses and all the prophets. That might have taken several days. Jesus probably summarized to reveal to these men who was walking among them.

Philip probably did the same when he was talking to the Ethiopian eunuch (Acts 8), or Stephen on the day he was stoned (Acts 6), or Peter on the day of Pentecost (Acts 2). They each used the narrative of the Scriptures to reveal God's message to the people.

The plan of redemption is itself a story: creation, fall, redemption, and fulfillment. Our very lives carry this story. Which parts will we tell? As Jesus demonstrated through His own life, stories serve a specific purpose. They're not just for children. They're not just for entertainment or filler. Stories provide context and characters so we can identify with them.

The truth connected with everyday life makes the best stories, and stories allow us to discover this truth for ourselves. The questions we ask, the imagery we use, and the language we utilize all serve to tell this story well.

LEARNING EFFECTIVE LAY LEADERSHIP IN THE CHURCH

JIM DEVRIES

Rick and I debated about including anything about lay leadership in this book because we wanted its emphasis to be on serving in the workplace, not in the church. But if you're leading in the workplace, you're likely to be "drafted" into helping in your church (or a parachurch organization). So here we've included some of the things I've learned through my experiences as a lay leader.

Ideally, local churches are about praying for others, gaining spiritual strength, help in resisting temptation and persecution, and finding community. They represent Christ in a visible form to the world through the actions of their members as they gather for teaching, worship, and prayer.

How is leading within a church or parachurch setting different from leading in a business? I learned most of my leadership experience and organization skills by working in enterprises and parachurch organizations, and I saw little if any difference between the two in the way leaders made decisions.

James M. Boice, a respected Presbyterian pastor, had this somewhat cynical comment on decision making within the local church:

> One of the things Presbyterians especially do is to outvote the dissenters. We call a meeting. We ask people to speak. We make a motion, being careful to follow *Robert's Rules of Order*. Then when we have our motion and our second, we vote to cut off debate, vote, and the majority prevails. Our will is done, and everything has been accomplished democratically. Who can complain? The losers have to keep quiet because the decision has been made. Unfortunately they do not keep quiet, and ruptures still occur. I have heard people say, "The Holy Spirit speaks through the fifty-one percent vote." But that is usually not the case, judging by the outcomes.[1]
>
> The church is unique, so it should operate differently from businesses. The church is spiritual and temporarily based here on earth and in its glory in heaven in the future, but businesses focus on man and his physical accomplishments. The table on the next page shows areas of contrast between the two.

The governance model God designed for the church is to have a plurality of leaders. Paul routinely appointed elders in the churches he founded,[3] and he also directed Titus to appoint leaders. Note the plural form in every town (church).[4] A plurality of leaders is needed because God's church is always under attack from within and without.

The writer of Acts records Paul giving these directions to the leaders of the Ephesian church:

THE CHURCH	BUSINESS
Created by God	Created by man
Plurality of coleaders	Single principal leader
Exists for eternity	Temporary
Head is Jesus Christ [2]	Head is man
Motive is love	Motive is gain
Spiritual focus	Material focus
True equality of people	Deliberate inequality
Values grace	Values works
Goal is to multiply	Goal is to monopolize
Value in diversity	Value in uniformity
Requires total allegiance	Requires partial allegiance

Pay careful attention to yourselves and to all the flock, in which the Holy Spirit has made you overseers, to care for the church of God, which he obtained with his own blood. I know that after my departure fierce wolves will come in among you, not sparing the flock; and from among your own selves will arise men speaking twisted things, to draw away the disciples after them.[5]

The plurality of leaders is needed because a church with only a single leader is in danger of attack. God desires a plurality of leaders in the local church to prevent one person's or one group's belief system from affecting an entire church.

Unfortunately, this has happened with some regularity. As additional protection, this team of leaders should reflect the congregation's composition and not be selected from an affinity group with a common background, conversion experience, education, or economic status. God's church has little to do with affinity groups.

When I was serving as an elder in my local church, I grew to appreciate the wisdom God gave to a diverse group of elders. The church's leaders need, first of all, to be spiritually mature. His design includes slave and free, rich and poor, educated and uneducated, the native and the alien—all unified by God's love.

What particular challenges does a Christ-centered leader face when leading within a church? What does he or she need to do?

CHOOSE PRAYER FIRST

In first Timothy 2:8, Paul says, "I want the men everywhere to pray, lifting up holy hands without anger or disputing" (NIV).

Everything we've discussed about prayer should be multiplied by seven when it comes to the church. Why do we choose to take action rather than pray? Why is it more comfortable as a leadership body to endlessly debate the mechanics of a proposed project than to pray?

J. Oswald Sanders explains why we may fail to pray:

A strange paradox, most of us find it hard to pray. We do not naturally delight in drawing near to God. We sometimes pay lip service to the delight and power of prayer. We call it indispensable; we know the Scriptures call for it. Yet we often fail to pray."[6]

Failure to pray in the church is deadly and can create spiritual havoc.

STRIVE FOR UNITY

Unity has immense power. When we live together in love and harmony, it can mean only one thing: each of us has ceased being our own lord and have submitted ourselves to *the* Lord. There can be no place for isolated individualism, the attitude Archbishop William Temple penned when he said, tongue-in-cheek, "I believe in one holy, infallible church, of which I regret to say that at present I am the only member."

In John 17, where Jesus prays to the Father, He says, "I in them and you in me—so that they may be brought to complete unity. Then the world will know that you sent me and have loved them even as you have loved me."[7]

In the book *Deepening Your Conversation with God*, the authors say,

> Note that Jesus claims for His disciples a powerful unity. A power he gives only to the Holy Spirit, to no single person—the power to persuade the world that he is indeed the One sent from God, "to let the world know that you sent me." The most potent argument for the authority and identity of Jesus does not have to come from philosophers and theologians and apologists. It can come from the simplest of believers who will live together in the unity of the Holy Spirit!"[8]

How does this unity come about? Only by focused prayer both as a group and individually until the Holy Spirit brings harmony.

In the church I attend, we routinely postpone a less-than-unanimous decision until the next meeting, even if only one member has objected. And lobbying the objecting leader between meetings is strictly prohibited; this time is for individual prayer.

Sometimes it takes multiple meetings to reach a consensus, but typically, everyone agrees at the next meeting.

At the close of one meeting, the sole dissenter was strongly opposed to the proposed action. So we decided to each pray over the next week. I was apprehensive when I came to the next meeting, unsure how I should lead to help reach unity on the issue. But even before I called the meeting to order, this man quickly raised his hand and said, "We should go ahead. The Lord changed my mind this week."

BE A SHEPHERD

I think God created sheep just to have an illustration to use when teaching leadership within His church. Scripture talks about both good and bad shepherds.[9] The biblical image of a good shepherd caring for his flock is powerful—standing long hours ensuring its safety, leading it to fresh pasture and clear water, carrying the weak, seeking the lost, healing the wounded and sick. The image of the shepherd is one of intimacy, tenderness, concern, skill, hard work, suffering, and love. It's a subtle blend of authority and care and as much tenderness as toughness.

This quote from the book *Biblical Eldership* by Alexander Strauch shows most parishioners have a different expectation for their lay leaders:

> When most Christians hear of church elders, they think of an official church board, lay officials, influential people within the local church, or advisors to the pastor. They think of elders as policymakers, financial officers, fund raisers, or administrators. They don't expect church elders to teach the Word or be involved pastorally in the lives of people.[10]

Being a shepherd within the church requires determination and steadfastness. God places people in your church, but not all are warm and huggable, not all are thankful, and not all are willing to go along with the desires of the rest of the church.

VALUE VOLUNTEERS

Volunteers require you to sharpen your skills in leading. They need to be recruited and then made to feel appreciated.

First, you need to repeatedly exhibit gratitude to your volunteers. Few things are more demotivating for anyone than to feel as if their work doesn't matter. Their feeling unappreciated is the fastest way to lose them. Thanking each volunteer often is crucial to their survival and growth within the church!

Other actions that can damage your ability to recruit and retain volunteers are lack of communication and lack of empowerment.

SHOW GRACE

Perceived rules rob us of joy, create strong divisions between followers of Christ, and repulse those who have not yet come to the knowledge of Him. Yet we allow rules to permeate our churches.

A simple message in the Bible says, "If you confess with your mouth that Jesus is Lord and believe in your heart that God raised him from the dead, you will be saved."[11] However, instead of accepting that simple message, we, like the Pharisees, start adding to the list. We pile on our convictions and preferences and then proceed to argue about them with other members of Christ's body. The more things we can check off for our side of the argument, the better we feel.

The church stagnates because its leaders become so preoccupied with the idea that they or another member of the organization will fail to live up to one of the "rules" and offend a fellow member. This kind of culture lacks grace.

As you allocate your time as a lay leader, does the church constitution take precedent? Or the hurting spouse who has just heard about their partner's infidelity? The early church stumbled over retaining the laws placed on Jewish believers because some members felt they were more important than unity.

VALUE GENEROSITY RATHER THAN ACCUMULATION

Although as church leaders we typically spend more time looking at financial reports and trying to control expenses, so we're viewed as "good" stewards, a church thrives on generosity.

Our pastor was preaching through the book of John, and the next Sunday he planned to preach on this story from chapter 12:

> Mary therefore took a pound of expensive ointment made from pure nard, and anointed the feet of Jesus and wiped his feet with her hair. The house was filled with the fragrance of the perfume. But Judas Iscariot, one of his disciples (he who was about to betray him), said, "Why was this ointment not sold for three hundred denarii and given to the poor?"[12]

He called me, and after explaining that the point of his upcoming sermon was that Mary was generous in her gift to Jesus and expected nothing in return, he made an unusual suggestion: "What if we announce that we'll be taking an *extra* offering the following week? We'll provide an opportunity for our congregation to give a generous thank-you gift to Jesus, promising it will be kept separate from our regular funds and be used to demonstrate generosity in some way."

I told him I thought that was a tremendous idea and that I would get the necessary approvals.

The overwhelming response was approximately four times the amount normally collected—and that was on top of the regular offering, which was the usual amount. But then we as leaders struggled for six months to determine how to use the funds in a way that would continue to demonstrate generosity. After much prayer, we found a use that continues to thank Jesus regularly. We built a prayer garden, where anyone could pray and meditate, and we have seen many wonderous answers to prayer as a result.

Yes, we had a few grumblers about wasting money ("No one needs a prayer garden to pray!"), but one of the biggest opponents recently asked for an opportunity to speak at a service and tell his story about how he was wrong to grumble. He had seen, in his words, "a miraculous change" in his life as a result of what had been done in thanks to Jesus.

GUARD AGAINST OFFENSIVE SPEECH

I remember a wonderful family of believers who left our church because of a careless word by one of our leaders. This quotation expands on the idea of guarding one's tongue.

> One of God's attributes is that He is slow to anger, so His stewards must also be slow to anger. Man's anger is a hindrance to the work of God, "for the anger of a man does not achieve the righteousness of God" (James 1:20). Since an elder [leader] must deal with people and their problems, a "hothead" will quickly find much material to fuel his anger. Proverbs warns against the perils of an angry man: "An angry man stirs up strife, a hot-tempered man abounds in transgression" (Proverbs 29:22). With his ugly, angry words, a quick-tempered man will destroy the peace and unity of God's family. The fierce looks and

harsh words of the quick-tempered man [or woman] will tear people apart emotionally, leaving people sick and destroyed in spirit. So a man who desires to be a church shepherd must be patient and self-controlled.[13]

REALIZE LEADERSHIP STYLE MATTERS

We've been studying Christ-centered leadership as it applies to our call to serve in a secular organization. If we're serving in one of these organizations, we serve Christ as our primary responsibility. However, we also have a secondary responsibility to work toward fulfilling the purpose of the organization itself.

The similar style of management for a local church has these seven distinguishing characteristics.

1. The leader values relationships and influence over control and positional authority.
2. The leader's focus is on function rather than titles.
3. The primary role of the leader is to serve others.
4. Any top-down leadership structure and mentality in the church significantly damages its culture.
5. Church growth will be in all the nations of the world, requiring leaders to be sensitive to the local culture of the church.
6. Leadership in the church seeks common ownership by inviting thoughtful engagement with staff for insights and diverse perspectives.
7. Every leader is accountable to every other leader. In times of friction, the church welcomes respectful disagreement.

EXERCISE LOVE

Love is not optional. Demonstrating love for others, particularly in times of personal adversity, can be a struggle. After washing His disciples' feet, Jesus told them, "A new commandment I give to you, that you love one another: just as I have loved you, you also are to love one another. By this all people will know that you are my disciples, if you have love for one another."[14]

CARE FOR LEADERS

Who cares for the church leaders? The members of the church should be caring for them. But unless those members have been leaders themselves, they may not understand some of pressures and joys leaders face.

Ask another lay leader or two to join you regularly in prayer for each other, the pastor, and associated church staff. Be authentic. Candidly ask for help in the areas where you struggle. Listen to the other leaders and offer help when requested or needed.

God gave Judy and me the privilege of starting a ministry to pastors and missionaries. We held two or more retreats each year in nice resorts for them and included their spouses if they were married. Their church or organization was asked to contribute a nominal amount, so their attendance wouldn't be counted as vacation time.

Quite frankly, although there was always teaching, the primary purpose was to spoil everyone a little bit and to give these couples some time away from church and family. Some of the topics addressed were stress and burnout, boundaries, health, exercise, and nutrition. Sometimes couples expressed it had been years since they had had an opportunity to be by themselves for an extended time just to share and be together. These are some needs these pastors and their spouses regularly expressed, which you as a church leader need to be aware of.

PROTECTION AND ACCOUNTABILITY

Church leaders need to protect their pastors, especially when it comes to rumors and gossip. Unfortunately, gossip and false accusations exist. But Paul told the Corinthian church, "Every charge must be established by the evidence of two or three witnesses."[15]

Deal with gossip quickly, because it flies on wings. Gossip damages leaders more than it damages members. Paul built in protection for the leaders by requiring that a charge must meet certain criteria even before it is to be considered by other leaders. Those bringing a charge must agree to abide by the decision of the leaders after their investigation and agree not to share an accusation with others.

Remind the leaders with whom you serve of Paul's admonition in Titus: "As for a person who stirs up division, after warning him once and then twice, have nothing more to do with him."[16]

Church leaders should also establish a small group of leaders to walk alongside the pastor and meet with him or her monthly not only to protect them from the stresses of ministry and to confidentially discuss other issues that may arise, but to hold them accountable as necessary. The pastor should be allowed to choose the majority of the members of the group, and their spouse should be asked to join the meeting occasionally to share any concerns they may have.

This group should be guarding the pastor's physical and mental health to prevent the possibility of excessive stress and burnout. Be ever alert to their needs. Sometimes additional help and special prayer is needed. Watch, listen, and observe with empathy, particularly for the spiritual warfare that can harass them. Be slow to judge!

REALISTIC EXPECTATIONS

Pastors—particularly pastors of small churches—have expectations placed on them by the other leaders in the church, every church member, and the community. Even their families have expectations. And sometimes the most difficult expectations to manage are their own! We see some of that reflected in the advice Ed Bratcher gave in our chapter that covered learning to delegate.

Church leaders need to clearly state their expectations for their pastor and come to agreement. Then they need to intervene when church members or anyone else attempts to demand more than agreed.

COMPENSATION

As I mentioned earlier, leaders are often reluctant to pray. Yet they find it easy to dig into areas that are concrete. One of these areas is church finances. A governing board is successful if the budget is balanced. But expenses like mortgages, utilities, insurance, and maintenance in most instances are fixed and don't provide much flexibility if there is a budget shortfall. So what expense becomes a target? Staff salaries.

If your church is part of a larger denomination, it most likely has some guidelines or even established wages, but that doesn't let the local leaders off the hook as far as I'm concerned. These two verses address wages:

> Let the elders who rule well be considered worthy of double honor, especially those who labor in preaching and teaching.[17]
>
> Look! The wages you failed to pay the workers who mowed your fields are crying out against you. The cries of the harvesters have reached the ears of the Lord Almighty.[18]

The second verse sometimes keeps me awake at night—from a business perspective but particularly in the church setting. If no denominational help for church leaders is available, you might look at the salary ranges for public school teachers with an equivalent degree to the pastor's education.

Local church leaders are responsible to ensure that the pastor is generously paid and his or her needs are met, particularly if they have unusual financial needs in the family, such as specialized education or specialized health care.

Church leaders should also be the only decision makers for a salary amount. There is nothing more humiliating for a pastor than having their salary become a matter of public debate!

AUTHORITY OVER STAFF AND VOLUNTEERS

One person, usually the pastor or executive pastor, should clearly be in charge of staff and volunteers. Church members, particularly those who volunteer in an area of ministry, can begin to think they have authority over the staff. If not addressed, this leads to confusion and discouragement for both the volunteer and the staff member. So make that authority clear.

APPRECIATION

In chapter 13 we talked about the revolutionary effect of appreciation in the workplace. If almost everyone you met with wanted something from you, wouldn't you appreciate a thank-you? A visit starting with, "No problem, Pastor. Just stopped by to tell you I appreciated your message Sunday. And by the way, Mrs. Smith let me know you were wonderful when you visited with her while she was sick.

"Also, we leaders think you will need a few extra days' rest after Lent, so we arranged for a weekend away for you and your family at your favorite vacation spot. We've even arranged for someone to fill the pulpit that Sunday. Have a good week!"

Don't be surprised if the pastor passes out at the shock! Positive messages are the exception. Show your appreciation and encourage others to join you!

I've struggled with all these issues. But I pray my experiences and the lessons I learned as God allowed me to serve in His church are helpful for those of you He also calls into lay leadership.

ACKNOWLEDGMENTS

To my longsuffering wife Judy who spent hours reading and re-reading the manuscript right up to the end. And to Tina, Rick's wife, for sharing Rick as he spent time on the road so the two of us could meet and share ideas.

To Rick for suggesting my story was worth sharing and encouraging me to continue when discouraged and things seemed to drag. In addition to writing, he helped me crystalize my thoughts and beliefs about the importance of Christ-centered leadership.

I am indebted to mentors like Bernie from the grocery store, Dick Sarns, and my business partners Ron Williams and Hugh Cummings in particular.

Rick would like to thank David Muir, his dear friend Colin Buckland, and above all, his dad as being key to his development as a leader.

Thanks to Michelle Sessoms who generously wrote the section on Learning from Jesus, the Master Communicator and let us share it with you.

We would be negligent if we didn't heartily thank Jean Kavich Bloom our freelance editor who took our thoughts and organized them so they made a logical presentation. But, most of all made them come alive and easy to read! And to Vanessa Carroll who did a wonderful job finding all of those little gremlins that creep in whenever you lift your eyes from the computer monitor and stretch.

ABOUT THE AUTHORS

JIM DEVRIES

Jim graduated from the University of Michigan with a degree in mechanical engineering. He worked for Sarns Inc., now a part of Terumo Medical Corporation, Baxter Laboratories, and Medtronic Incorporated. He is an entrepreneur, inventor, and sculptor, who founded DLP, Inc. He received the Entrepreneur of the Year Award in 1992, presented jointly by Ernst and Young, Inc. Magazine, and Merrill Lynch. A doctor of Letters from Grand Rapids Theological Seminary in 2005 and the University of Michigan, College of Engineering, Alumni Merit Award in 2012. His website is www.jhdevries.com.

MICHELLE SESSOMS

Michelle is the Director of International Field Ministries for Freedom to Lead International®. Michelle has been a missionary, educator, cross-cultural trainer, administrator, and writer. She holds a Master of Arts in Intercultural Studies. Michelle has spent significant time living in East Africa, Central Asia, and Southeast Asia. After a decade being involved in campus ministry at universities across China, she now resides in North Carolina. (Yes, she is Rick and Tina's daughter.)

RICK SESSOMS

Rick is founder and CEO of Freedom to Lead International®, a non-profit entity that uses story, images, and music to cultivate Christ-centered leaders. He has been a missionary, pastor, and educator, and has coached leaders and provided consultation for ministry organizations throughout the Americas, Africa, Europe, North Asia, South Asia, and Oceania. He has an MDiv, a DMin, and a PhD in organizational leadership. He formerly served as chair of the Lausanne Leadership Development Working Group. Rick and his wife, Tina, have two grown children.

OTHER PUBLICATIONS
BY THE AUTHORS

JIM DEVRIES

James H DeVries, *Work, Wealth, Wisdom, & Worship*
(Grand Rapids, MI: Self-Published, 2020)
ISBN: 97986535330760 paperback

RICK SESSOMS

Rick Sessoms, *Leading with Story: Cultivating Christ-Centered Leaders in a Storycentric Generation*
(Pasadena, CA: William Carey Library, 2016)
ISBN: 9780878085309 paperback
ISBN: 08780853300 eBook

ENDNOTES

INTRODUCTION

1   John 6:38

2   Hebrews 1:3

3   John 14:9

4   Jeremiah 25:9

5   Henri J.M. Nouwen, *The Path of Waiting* (New York, NY: The Crossway Publishing Co., 1955), 33–35.

6   Matthew 26:42

CHAPTER 1

1   Matthew 5:16

2   1 Corinthians 15:23–25

3   Luke 16:16

4   Paul Marshall, *Heaven Is Not My Home: Living in the Now of God's Creation* (Nashville, TN: Word Publishing, 1998), 243.

5   Matthew 6:19–21

6   Luke 6:35

7   Matthew 5:45

CHAPTER 2

1   Romans 8:28

2   Charles Frazier, *Varina* (3 Crows Corporation, 2018), eBook.

3   Matthew 22:36–40

4   Matthew 28:18–20

CHAPTER 3

1   Check out Freedom To Lead International's website for more information on this as well as on Christ-centered leadership: Freedomtolead.net.

2   Genesis 2:15

3   Mark 16:20

4   John 5:15–17

5   Acts 18:1–4

6   Hugh Whelchel, *How Then Should We Work? Rediscovering the Biblical Doctrine of Work* (McLean, VA: Institute for Faith Work, and Economics, 2012), 59–66.

7   Alister McGrath, "Calvin and the Christian Calling," *First Things* Vol. 94 (June/July 1999), 31–35.

8   Henri J. M. Nouwen, *The Path of Waiting* (New York, NY: Crossroad Publishing Co., 1995), 34–35.

9   McGrath, "Calvin and the Christian Calling."

10 Genesis 8:21–22

11 1 Chronicles 22

12 1 Chronicles 29:1

13 Exodus 36–40

14 Exodus 31:6

15 Psalm 8

16 Wayne Grudem, *Business for the Glory of God* (New York, NY: Crossway Publishing Co., 2003), 11–12.

17   For a more extensive presentation of the theology of work and its relationship with common grace, we suggest Hugh Whelchel's book *How Then Should We Work? Rediscovering the Biblical Doctrine of Work.* Available from the Institute for Faith, Work & Economics, 8400 Westpark Dr. Suite 100, McLean, VA, 22102.

18   John 17:4–5

19   Daniel 12:13

CHAPTER 4

1   Thanks to Mike Metzger, President of the Clapham Institute, who explained a clear way to present these concepts! RS

2   Genesis 1:28

3   Genesis 2:19

4   John 5:17

5   Luke 4:18–19

6   Colossians 1:15–23

7   Luke 19:10

8   Colossians 1:19–20

9   Revelation 21:1–3

10   Rick Sessoms, "Leading with Excellence in Babylon," Freedom To Lead International, https://freedomtolead.net/leading-with-excellence-in-babylon/, March 2, 2020.

11   Jeremiah 29:4–7

12   Paul Rude, *Significant Work: Discover the Extraordinary Worth of What You Do Every Day* (Copper Center, Alaska: Everyday Significance [Publishers], 2013), 12.

13   Daniel 12:13

CHAPTER 5

1   Judges 6:15

2   Exodus 3:11

3   Jim Collins, *Good to Great* (New York: HarperCollins Publishers, 2001), 36.

4   Romans 12:8

5   John N. Oswalt, *The Book of Isaiah*, Chapters 1–39, The New International Commentary on the Old Testament, (Grand Rapids, MI: Eerdmans Publishing Co., 1986), 57.

6   Oswalt, *The Book of Isaiah*, 60.

PART II: ONE LEADER'S JOURNEY

1   Walter Brueggemann *The Message of the Psalms* (Minneapolis, MN: Augsburg Press, 1984), 15–23.

2   Romans 8:28

CHAPTER 7

1   Mark 10:29–30

2   Hebrews 13:1–2

3   Matthew 28:16–19

CHAPTER 8

1   Romans 8:28

2   Keith Miller, *The Taste of New Wine*, 5th Edition (Orleans, MA: Paraclete Press, 1995)

3   William J. Petersen and Randy Petersen, *100 Books That Changed the Century* (Ada, MI: Revell, Baker Publishing Group, 2000).

CHAPTER 9

1   Amos 5:19 NET
2   Psalm 40:1–3

CHAPTER 10

1   Genesis 39:2–6
2   Genesis 39:2, 23
3   Genesis 50:24
4   Hebrews 11:22
5   Tom Paterson, *Living the Life You Were Meant to Live* (Nashville, TN: Thomas Nelson, 1998).
6   Both can be seen on jhdevries.com along with some of my other work.
7   If you're interested in a full story of the foundation, Google the foundation's name.
8   Numbers 6:24–26
9   Romans 8:28
10   Micah 6:8

PART III: CREATING A HEALTHY CULTURE

1   Michael Munford and Yitzhack Fried, "Give them what they want or give them what they need?" Ideology in the study of leadership (Journal of Organizational Behavior, Vol 35, 2014), 622–634.

CHAPTER 11

1   1 Thessalonians 5:17
2   Psalm 18:11
3   Psalm 18:6
4   1 Kings 19:10

5   Hebrews 1:3

6   1 Corinthians 13:12

CHAPTER 12

1   John 17:20–23

CHAPTER 13

1   Nikos Androitis, "The 5 Real Reasons Why Good Employees Quit," efront blog 2018/02, efrontlearning.com, https://www.efrontlearning.com/blog/?s=5+real+reasons.

2   Victor Lipman, "66% of Employees Would Quit If They Feel Unappreciated," *Forbes*, April 15, 2017, https://www.forbes.com/sites/victorlipman/2017/04/15/66-of-employees-would-quit-if-they-feel-unappreciated/?sh=2cd7f8936897.

3   1 Thessalonians 5:18

4   Psalm 105:1

5   1 Corinthians 15:33

6   John 16:8

7   Matthew 7:1–5

8   Matthew 7:6. Jesus is addressing a Jewish audience. Because both dogs and pigs are associated with Gentiles it is likely this verse is referring to a nonbeliever. JDV

CHAPTER 14

1   Psalm 46:10

2   Phoenix Seminary, IS517 Narrative in Ministry: Engaging Millennials and Diverse Audiences.

3   D. Bruce Seymour, *Creating Stories That Connect* (Grand Rapids, MI: Kregel, 2007), 15–39.

4   Genesis 11:5–7

5   Zephaniah 3:9
6   John 2:18–22

CHAPTER 15
1   Exodus 16:2–3
2   Numbers 11:4–6

CHAPTER 16
1   Henri J.M. Nouwen, The Path of Waiting (New York, NY: The Crossroad Publishing Co., 1995), 35.
2   Matthew 19:16–22
3   Romans 12:11
4   John 2:13–17
5   Matthew 8:5–13
6   David John Seel Jr., *The New Copernicans* (Nashville, TN: Thomas Nelson Publishers, 2018).
7   Hebrews 11:39
8   Titus 3:10
9   Numbers 27:16–17
10   Deuteronomy 12:8–9
11   James 1:3–4
12   Psalm 63:3-4

CHAPTER 17
1   Proverbs 12:15 NIV
2   Wess Roberts, *Leadership Secrets of Attila the Hun* (New York, NY: Business Plus, 1987), 102.
3   Psalm 10:4 NIV
4   Micah 6:8
5   Daniel 4:37 NIV

6   Daniel 5:20 NIV

7   Luke 6:41

8   Luke 16:13–14

9   An observation that a person's sense of morality lessens as his or her power increases. The statement was made by Lord Acton, a British historian of the late nineteenth and early twentieth centuries.

10   Matthew 26:64

11   Micah 7:2–3 NIV

12   The name in this illustration has been changed.

13   This occurred directly after God renewed the covenant that Isaac would have numerous ancestors like the grains of sand on the seashore.

14   Genesis 26:6–11

15   Romans 8:28

16   1 John 4:18

17   This is a different product and a different competitor than the ones involving a lawsuit in chapter 8.

18   Matthew 5:25–26

19   James 1:19–20

20   Romans 12:19

CHAPTER 18

1   Colossians 3:12–14 NIV

2   2 Peter 1:5–9

3   God said through Isaiah, "'For a brief moment I deserted you, but with great compassion I will gather you. In overflowing anger for a moment I hid my face from you, but with everlasting love I will have compassion on you,' says the LORD, your Redeemer" (Isaiah 54:7–8).

4   God said to Hosea, "Yet it was I who taught Ephraim [Israel] to walk; I took them up by their arms, but they did not know that I healed them. I led them with cords of kindness, with the bands of love, and I became to them as one who eases the yoke on their jaws, and I bent down to them and fed them" (Hosea 11:3–4).

5   Titus 3:4–5

6   Proverbs 11:2

7   Philippians 2:3

8   Matthew 11:29; 2 Chronicles 7:14

9   Exodus 33:11

10   Numbers 12:3

11   Matthew 21:4–5

12   1 Kings 19:11–12

13   Genesis 6:13

14   Mark 16:7

15   Luke 17:3–4

16   Isaiah 43:25; Hebrews 8:12, 10:17; Jeremiah 31:34; Acts 3:19

17   1 Corinthians 13:4–7

18   John 13:34–35

19   Luke 20:46–47

20   Habakkuk 2:14

21   James 1:5

22   1 Corinthians 9:24–26

CHAPTER 19

1   Matthew 23:23–24

2   Jeremiah 17:9

3   You may want to Google the term *satisfactory underperformance*, which is a whole field of leadership in its own right.

CLOSING THOUGHTS

1   Romans 8:28

2   Psalm 1:1–3

3   Numbers 6:24–26

LEARNING TO COMMUNICATE RESPONSIBLY

1   A few years ago Rick wrote a four-part series of blog articles that contained many of these ideas. To find them, go to: https://freedomtolead.net/resources/christ-centered-leadership/responsible-listener.

2   Philippians 2:4

3   Matthew 7:1–2 NIV

LEARNING FROM JESUS, THE MASTER COMMUNICATOR

1   The Orality Institute is now operational and has students enrolled.

2   Matthew 22:19

3   Matthew 22:22

4   Matthew 18:5–6

5   Luke 9:18

6   Luke 9:19

7   Luke 9:20

8   Duane Elmer, *Cross-Cultural Servanthood: Serving the World in Christlike Humility* (Westmont, IL: InterVarsity Press, 2009), 164.

9   Luke 24:27

LEARNING EFFECTIVE LAY LEADERSHIP IN THE CHURCH

1   James Montgomery Boice, *An Expository Commentary, Acts* (Grand Rapids, MI: Baker, 2002), 113.

2   Scripture tells us that Christ is the head of the church: "He put all things under his feet and gave him as head over all things to the church, which is his body, the fullness of him who fills all in all" (Ephesians 1:22–23).

3   Acts 14:23

4   Titus 1:5

5   Acts 20:28–30

6   J. Oswald Sanders, *Spiritual Leadership* (Chicago, IL: Moody Publishers, 2007), 83.

7   John 17:23 NIV

8   B. Patterson and D. L. Goetz, *Deepening Your Conversation with God* (Minneapolis, MN: Bethany House Publishers, 2001), 162.

9   Zechariah 11:15–16

10   Alexander Strauch, *Biblical Eldership* (Colorado Springs, CO: Lewis & Roth Publishers, 1995), 15.

11   Romans 10:9

12   John 12:3–5

13   Alexander Strauch, *Biblical Eldership* (Colorado Spring, CO: Lewis & Roth Publishers, 1995), 232.

14   John 13:34–35

15   2 Corinthians 13:1

16   Titus 3:10

17   1 Timothy 5:17

18   James 5:4 NIV